1 9 9 1

THE GRAYWOLF

SHORT FICTION SERIES

ALSO EDITED BY DOROTHY SENNETT

Full Measure: Modern Short Stories on Aging

Vital Signs

International Stories on Aging

✳   ✳   ✳   ✳   ✳

EDITED BY DOROTHY SENNETT

WITH ANNE CZARNIECKI

INTRODUCTION BY

ROBERTSON DAVIES

GRAYWOLF PRESS / SAINT PAUL

The editor gratefully acknowledges the grant from the Margaret S. Mahler Institute of the Gray Panthers which made this anthology possible. Further support has been provided by the Minnesota State Arts Board, with funds provided through an appropriation by the Minnesota State Legislature, and by the National Endowment for the Arts. Graywolf Press is the recipient of a McKnight Foundation Award administered by the Minnesota State Arts Board and receives generous contributions from corporations, foundations, and individuals. Graywolf Press is a member agency of United Arts, Saint Paul.

Published by G R A Y W O L F P R E S S
2402 University Avenue, Suite 203
Saint Paul, Minnesota   55114
All rights reserved

9 8 7 6 5 4 3 2
First printing, 1991

Library of Congress Cataloging-in-Publication Data

Vital signs : international stories on aging / edited by Dorothy
Sennett with Anne Czarniecki ; introduction by Robertson Davies.
    p.   cm.   — (The Graywolf short fiction series)
      I S B N 1-55597-143-1 : $12.95
1. Aging – Fiction. 2. Short stories. I. Sennett, Dorothy, 1909-
    II. Czarniecki, Anne D. III. Series.
        PN6120.95.A48V5   1991
        808.83'1 – dc20   90-24675

TABLE OF CONTENTS

Dorothy Sennett / *Preface* / vii

Robertson Davies / *Introduction* / xi

I

Hennie Aucamp / *Soup for the Sick* / 3

Jonathan Kariara / *Her Warrior* / 7

Charles Mungoshi / *The Setting Sun and the Rolling World* / 13

II

Toshio Mori / *The Man with Bulging Pockets* / 21

Leslie Marmon Silko / *Humaweepi, the Warrior Priest* / 27

Alice Walker / *To Hell with Dying* / 35

III

Ruth Prawer Jhabvala / *The Man with the Dog* / 45

Yasunari Kawabata / *The Neighbors* / 67

Zhang Jie / *An Unfinished Record* / 72

IV

Mohammed Khudayyir / *Clocks Like Horses* / 89

Amos Oz / *The Way of the Wind* / 104

Alifa Rifaat / *Telephone Call* / 128

V

Maurice Gee / *A Glorious Morning, Comrade* / 135

Elizabeth Jolley / *Pear Tree Dance* / 144

VI

Margareta Ekström / *Lilies of the Valley* / 157

Mavis Gallant / *His Mother* / 167

Francesca Sanvitale / *The Electric Typewriter* / 181

Tatyana Tolstaya / *Okkervil River* / 190

VII

Jorge Luis Borges / *The Immortals* / 205

Jamaica Kincaid / *My Mother* / 211

Julio Ricci / *The Concert* / 217

✳   ✳   ✳   ✳   ✳

Preface

✳   ✳   ✳   ✳   ✳

*V*ITAL SIGNS is a sequel that follows the publication of *Full Measure: Modern Short Stories on Aging* (edited by Dorothy Sennett, Graywolf Press, 1988). The warm response to *Full Measure* revealed considerable public interest in the ways that gifted modern writers see old people. Like its predecessor, this book attempts to defeat the stereotyping of old people (ageism) through the immediacy of the short story.

As in the earlier book, the central character in each story is a contemporary old man or old woman. This time, however, I have gone farther afield. Although a few of the writers included here are American, my emphasis this time has been on writers from the rest of the world – for example, from Japan, China, Sweden, and Australia. *Vital Signs* is unique in its depiction of fictional old people from a variety of cultures. Many of these writers became known to me only through library research, and I hope this collection will offer them new audiences.

In no story is the protagonist meant to portray a class. (Zhang Jie's old Chinese professor in "An Unfinished Record" is himself, uniquely.) What each of these writers intends, I think, is to give us a fleeting glimpse of reality at a certain time and place, and, from the effect of that time and place upon one old person, to make us sense a whole – often a whole lifetime. And, because a short story is built upon the most intimate aspects of a life, these homely details may light up not only a lifetime, but an entire milieu. How much we can learn of where and how aged people in the Soviet Union live from Tatyana Tolstaya's "Okkervil River"! In Hennie Aucamp's "Soup for the Sick" an old white woman in South Africa attempts to transcend racism by her manner of dying; her will provides that, if she can be buried beside a lifelong black friend, she will leave money for the building of a hospital.

Although one short story cannot describe a whole people, it can say something about that people's values. This collection, like *Full Measure*, tells us that, from country to country, old people survive in like ways. We survive in our attachment to living things, to places, to the pursuits we loved in our youth, and in our connections with those we love profoundly. These themes permeate the stories.

In "The Man with Bulging Pockets," Toshio Mori, a Japanese American, writing of the time of the Japanese internment camps in the United States, describes with sweetness and charm how an old man develops a friendship with one of the camp's young children, by way of coming to terms with his own confinement.

In "The Setting Sun and the Rolling World," Charles Mungoshi, a Zimbabwean writer, portrays the classic struggle between a father's devotion to the land and his son's determination to explore a broader world. We understand the father's pain and the son's inevitable breaking-away.

Set in Budapest, Hungary, Mavis Gallant's "His Mother" explores intergenerational relationships in a Communist society. "She felt shamed because it had not been in her to control armies, history, his stony watery world...." She would have liked to visit her permanently absent son in Glasgow, bringing him family jewelry, family photographs, and a cake – all the requisites for absent sons.

I chose each writer not only for his or her great skill, but also as a representative of the culture from which the writer sprang. But, if you ascribe any instructional value to the stories, you proceed at your own risk. The message of a short story is implicit, not explicit. What any short story "means" is a feeling that arises from within the reader.

"Theme," John Gardner tells us in *The Art of Fiction*, "is not imposed on the story but evoked from within." To the limited extent that these imagined lives evoke real life, each writer directs a searchlight upon some formerly hidden corner of old age, as lived in a culture little known to us.

DOROTHY SENNETT

ROBERTSON   DAVIES

✳   ✳   ✳   ✳   ✳

*A*BOUT SIXTY YEARS AGO, I said to my father, "Old Mr. Senex is showing his age; he sometimes talks quite stupidly." My father replied, "That isn't age. He's always been stupid. He is just losing his ability to conceal it."

This astonished me, because Mr. Senex had been president of this and that, and the chairman of several boards, and had acquired a good deal of money and the esteem that goes with it. But I thought about what my father had said, and gradually understood that Mr. Senex, in earlier days, had possessed enough conventional wisdom, enough ordinary savvy, enough of those qualities that made him acceptable to people like himself, to make a very fair mark in the world in which he moved. But what sort of world was that?

IT WAS NOT a world in which I was interested. Even as a very young man – indeed, as a boy – I had a bee in my bonnet about theater history, which has subsequently been one of my principal enthusiasms and pursuits. I had asked Mr. Senex if he had seen any of the great players of his younger days, and what he had thought about them. Oh yes, he had seen Irving a couple of times, and Ellen Terry with him. Yes, he had seen Forbes-Robertson as Hamlet. He had once seen Mrs. Pat Campbell, whom he recalled as a beautiful woman. He had seen Sarah Bernhardt; she was a thin woman. He had seen some early Shaw, and did not think much of it; too talky. He had seen

Charley's Aunt when it was still fairly new; very funny. He had always been a theater-goer. But he did not remember anything in revealing detail about any of these people. Mr. Senex had seen all sorts of interesting and exciting things, and sometimes he had even beheld greatness, but Mr. Senex had not been moved, or touched. It was Mr. Senex's assumption of intellectual superiority to Bernard Shaw that made me suspect that he was stupid. I abandoned Mr. Senex; I brooded on my father's sharp assessment; Mr. Senex's old age was truly the summing-up of what he had been.

Was I unjust to Mr. Senex? Many years later, when I had become a newspaper editor, now and then I used to say to a reporter, "There's a person at such-and-such an address who will be a hundred next week. Go and see what emerges about the past century." Never, in all those years, did a reporter return with anything worth more than six inches of stuff that might have been written without questioning the old person, who had been untouched by anything except personal affairs of the most commonplace kind. I composed in my head a piece that would have done for any of these centenarians:

> *Mr./Mrs. – – – – – has completed a century of life during which he/she has suffered the usual childhood diseases, undergone the education provided by the state without discernible effect, married and replenished the earth with two and one-half children, and is now visited from time to time by seven and one-quarter grandchildren and three great-grandchildren, one of whom is in utero; has never touched alcohol/counsels moderation; eschews tobacco/still loves his/her pipe; has consumed and extruded a hundred and nine thousand, five hundred pounds of aliment (approx.); can still read without glasses and never misses an issue of this newspaper; legs going and cannot walk farther than the gate. Thinks*

*people used to work harder and save. Cannot abide this
modern music. Has never seen or met anyone of any interest and remembers nothing that is not personal. Advice
to the young: read a chapter of your Bible every day and
never eat tomatoes, which cause cancer (can't understand why these doctors don't catch on to it).*

Of course this sprang from the bitterness that is an occupa-
tional disease of editors. Not all old people can be so categorized,
though in my opinion far too many of them fit the description. I
have grown old myself, and have opinions about it, and about
my coevals. What ails most of them, and what has ailed them all
their lives, is that they lack curiosity. They have never engaged
themselves strongly in anything. The waters of life have washed
over them without anything soaking in. They are not interesting
when old because they were never interesting when young, or in
that portion of life that is described – God knows why – as "the
prime."

Curiosity, it appears to me, is the great preservative and the
supreme emollient. Not, of course, curiosity about theater history alone or at all, but curiosity about *something*. Enthusiasm.
Zest. That's what makes old age (forgive me; I must leave my
typewriter to throw up, for I have just heard someone use that
nauseating expression, "the twilight years" – ah, that feels better) a delight. One has seen so much, and one is eager to see
more. One has reached a few conclusions. The twilight years
(ugh!) are a glorious sundown.

Curiosity comes in many packages. For some people it is
simple gossip, but good gossip is fine stuff, and more people
ought to jot down what they hear. Posterity will be grateful.
Look at the homage we still pay, pay increasingly, to splendid
gossips like John Aubrey or Horace Walpole. People in the future will want to know what you paid for things, what you ate
and at what time of day, what the fashion in courting was, and

how much intimacy did people really expect before marriage; what funerals were like and what sort of jokes did people make at marriages; did you beat your wife/husband, and, if so, when, if ever, did you stop? History rests on a great heap of personal detail, and historians still wrangle as to whether Napoleon would have won at Waterloo if his hemorrhoids had not been killing him on June 18, 1815. We want to *know*. We want to know unflaggingly and tastelessly, and if we dared to ask our friends the questions that are uppermost in our minds we should probably be ostracized beyond hope of reprieve. That is why some of us confide to a diary or to letters such facts as we can glean, and the fantasies that arise from them. When we have lost our curiosity about our world we have lost much, though not all.

We have lost all when we cease to be curious about ourselves, for that means that we have indeed abandoned hope. When we succumb to the bodily and mental habits of those who have given up all hope of change or improvement we have lifted the latch of the tomb. It is not easy to fight this fight, for old age has its seductions. As Juliet remarks, with a wisdom beyond her years,

> . . . *Old folks, many feign as they were dead –*
> *Unwieldly, slow, heavy and pale as lead.*

We do it to claim and insist on the consideration we suppose is owing to our years; if we hobble and hesitate and make a fuss, we lend weight to behaviour and utterances that may not, truly considered, amount to very much. It is tempting to fall into these habits because temptation comes in many forms and does not abandon us as we grow old. Just as adolescence may lean on tears and petulance to get its way, old age may seize on a physical decay, which it is tempting to exaggerate. We shall grow slow and forgetful soon enough, without embracing and fostering the process.

Forgetful – yes indeed, the old forget. But so do the young. As

Dr. Johnson remarked, if a young man forgets where he has put his hat we think nothing of it, but if an old man does so, we exchange winks, and imagine that he is breaking up. To forget trifles is nothing; after all, we have seventy or more years of experience to keep in mind, sift, and explore, lest we sink into mental and spiritual constipation.

If we refuse to accept this kind of stupor, the intellectual and spiritual life in old age is active and even turbulent. The passions do not die; they change their direction. The poets who do not die young know it well and have said it well. Hear Thomas Hardy:

> *. . . Time, to make me grieve,*
> *Part steals, lets part abide;*
> *And shakes this fragile frame at eve*
> *With throbbings of noontide.*

Such throbbings must be handled with skill or they may bring disaster. How many great men, in old age, have found themselves painfully in love with a woman young enough to be a daughter or a granddaughter? Love may reassert itself in a passion of great intensity, and fasten upon someone who seems to bring again the fervor and freshness of youth. We must be mindful of the wisdom of Henrik Ibsen, whose affair with Emilie Bardach, whom he called "the May sun of a September life" was conducted with a discretion that was by no means youthful, but which enlarged the life of the old poet and the young woman. So also with Anthony Trollope and Kate Field. It cannot always be so, and Yeats' later affairs brought him pain and sometimes humiliation. We must be as wise as we can, and there is really no more to be said about it.

I speak only of men, but women too have these autumn blossomings, and are perhaps even more in danger than are men, for we are not greatly astonished when a man – even a great man – makes a fool of himself, but the spectacle of a woman in the toils of an ill-fated affair is deeply distressing for – whatever the feminists may say – we expect more good sense from them, forgetting that good sense may not always win the day.

Much advice has been given to the old, ranging from the high-minded stoicism of Cicero's *De Senectute* to the very personal adjurations Swift addresses to himself: "Not to be peevish, or morose, or suspicious...Not to be covetous...Not to neglect decency, or cleanliness for fear of falling into Nastyness...Not to be positive or opinionative"; good enough advice so far as it goes, but if one wishes to go further, into the truly important matters, I know of no book so valuable as *The Art of Growing Old* by that extraordinary, neglected genius John Cowper Powys, who followed his own advice to the age of ninety-two.

Says Powys: "If by the time we're sixty we haven't learnt what a knot of paradox and contradiction life is, and how exquisitely the good and bad are mingled in every action we take, and what a compromising hostess Our Lady of Truth is, we haven't grown old to much purpose. I suppose the hardest of all things to learn and the thing that most distinguishes what is called 'a ripe old age' is the knowledge that while bold uncritical action is necessary if things are to move at all, we are only heading for fresh disaster if some portion of our interior soul doesn't function in critical detachment, while we commit ourselves to the tide, keeping a weather-eye upon both horizons."

This passage might well have been written by C.G. Jung, whose writings on old age, which he experienced until he was eighty-six, return again and again to a favourite doctrine that he finds first in the philosophy of Heraclitus. It concerns the law that opposites tend, at last, to unite. But the unified opposites are not unchanged; they partake each of the character of the other, and so when youth runs at last into age, age partakes of much of the openness and receptiveness of youth, balancing this expansiveness of spirit with the experience that has been accumulated during a long life – keeping that weather-eye on both horizons, as Powys says.

In life, says Dr. Jung, we spend the first half of our span of years finding our place in the world, finding our sexual orientation, finding our appointed work, finding what things can serve us and what we must avoid or abjure. But by the age of forty or so we take a change of direction, and henceforward seek knowledge of the world and of mankind, and above all knowledge of ourselves; in the theological phrase, we "make up our souls" and this is the great achievement of the second half of life, and the achievement that makes death the completion of something that has become a unity, with a quality of achievement and significance for ourselves and those around us. This is what makes age not a burden and a defeat, but marvelously enjoyable in spite of the limitations of the aging body.

If this great work can be attempted and in some measure completed it brings gifts as handsome in their way as are the gifts of youth, which Powys calls the secret of life, contained in a certain quality in matter itself that must be called a humorous one. Not, he insists "ebullient ribaldry and exuberant bawdiness" but rather "a humour inherent in the System of Things, or, as I prefer to express it, in our present Dimension of the Multiverse, that exists quite apart from the humorist who reveals it, a humor that was there before he appeared and will be there when he has disappeared."

This is philosophical or perhaps metaphysical speculation that not everybody finds welcome. But what Powys says is contained in a Welsh folksong that has long been dear to me and that is called, in English (though I have never heard any Englishman sing it) *The Kind Old Man*.

The song tells of some boys – kind-hearted boys, but somewhat given to melancholy as the young often are – who meet an old man near a river. In a slow, lugubrious measure they ask him

xviii * *Vital Signs*

where he has been wandering? The tune changes abruptly to the major and a rapid time; the old man says he has been fishing. The boys, deeply sorry for his age and what seems to them to be his decrepitude, persist in their questioning; what did he catch? Oh, nothing much; a couple of flatfish. Why is the poor old soul so wet? What – oh, because he fell into the river. And why is he shivering? Because he is cold from his dowsing. What if he should die? Well, of course they'll bury him. And where would he like to be buried? Under the old hearthstone boys, nowhere else. But why beneath the hearthstone? So that he can hear the porridge bubble – and the old man has answered every question in his merry, dancing tune.

Here is the unity of the opposites indeed. And here is the humor inherent in the System of Things. We would not wish the boys a whit less kind or solicitous, and we would not wish the old man any less merry in his acceptance of what must be.

In the stories that follow, as in the preceding volume called *Full Measure*, old age is explored through a number of special sensibilities. The fact that such volumes as these are called for is evidence of modern determination to come to terms with a state of life which, once reserved for the few, is now the expectation of the many.

FOR ESTHER AND NORMAN BROWN

I

Soup for the Sick

✳   ✳   ✳   ✳   ✳

Hennie Aucamp has published many volumes of short fiction in Afrikaans, and is acknowledged as the leading exponent of short fiction in Afrikaans literature. He lectures in education at the University of Stellenbosch in South Africa.

*T*ANT RENSIE went to her rest years ago, but she remains one of the most fascinating people I remember from my childhood. Fascinating, not for what we knew of her, but for what we suspected about her. In reality she was not an exceptional person, she was retiring, although not a hermit. She regularly attended church functions and fêtes, and from time to time she visited the Scottish doctor or old Mr. and Mrs. Verwey. But this was very occasionally, and later not at all. Her health troubled her.

She would have no help from outside. Sofietjie, her life-long nurse and friend, was sufficient for her. Even when it began to look as if her end was near, no family came to visit. Twenty years before that, she and Sofietjie had arrived in our Karoo dorp and had moved into the tower house that stood on the edge of town. Even then she had received no family visits. Had she renounced her family, or had they disowned her? Perhaps they had parted by mutual agreement?

Whoever tried to talk to Tant Rensie about her past came up

against the barrier of her mysterious smile, and anyone trying to break through that barrier laid himself open to insult or permanent dismissal.

It later became general knowledge in Klipkraal that one shouldn't pry into Tant Rensie's past. Only strangers fell into that trap. Nonetheless people remained inquisitive: Perhaps she had been born in another country? Perhaps she had come to South Africa for health reasons? Something in her speech and her way of keeping house marked her as different.... Something – and here they whispered about the thing that vaguely disturbed the whole of Klipkraal – there was something different about her relationship with Sofietjie....

One shouldn't be so intimate with one's servant. It wasn't that they were familiar, or that they chattered to each other. It was just that each was so aware of the other. If Sofietjie appeared, as quietly as a cat, in the doorway, Tant Rensie knew it even if she sat with her back towards her. "Tea," she would say to Sofietjie, and Sofietjie would glide back into the dim passage as if absorbed into it. To tell the truth their exchanges were brief, even curt. Sofietjie knew her place, as the older people would say. Nevertheless there was something between them.

On one particular evening I became very aware of the silent relationship between Tant Rensie and Sofietjie. It was the occasion that I first saw Sofietjie step out of line. Tant Rensie had been ailing for some time, more frequently in bed that out of it. Ma, who was the district nurse, sent me with a pot of soup to Tant Rensie's house.

When nobody answered the door I simply walked in, since the front door was ajar. Tant Rensie's bedroom door was also open, and Sofietjie sat on the bed next to Tant Rensie with her brown hands folded protectively over Tant Rensie's. Two old people, both grey-haired, the one white and serene, the other brown.

They were whispering confidentially to each other, but when they became aware of me they stopped talking and looked up calmly, innocently.

"Oh, Stevie, soup," Tant Rensie tried to prop herself up against the pillows.

"Partridge soup," I reported with pride. "I shot it myself."

Tant Rensie struggled against the cushions.

"Slowly now, your heart," Sofietjie said sharply.

"Not my heart, yours, Sofie. You are not to lift me again!"

Sofietjie smiled gently. I had never seen her severe face look so beautiful. She was also wrinkled, she had many wrinkles if one looked closely, but she seemed much younger than Tant Rensie. She didn't look like any of the coloured people I knew. Her nose was delicately formed, her mouth proud, and her eyes, with dark shadows beneath them, glowed.

"Go and fetch plates and spoons for all of us, Sofie. . . ."

Flustered, I protested when a short while later Sofie offered me a plate. I had already eaten.

"Just be sociable," coaxed Tant Rensie. "Go on."

Sofie sat once more on the bed, calmly holding a soup plate in her capable hand.

Why did Tant Rensie act so strangely? Had I become the embodiment of the social order that she had resisted so passively for so many years? A heavy burden for a twelve-year-old boy! Or did she want to "educate" me? Or had she simply become too old and tired to bother about any social code?

That afternoon still holds timelessness for me in just the way that moments of revelation are timeless. Through the green curtains the light, cool as in an aquarium, filtered into Tant Rensie's room. Unexpectedly one smelt roses – in the room or outside in the garden? They must have been in the room. It was a heavy perfume, pervasive and almost like decay. Suddenly I knew that between these two people was a bond beyond my apprehension. I was strung taut, needing to push my intuition further than my years allowed.

Sofietjie died before Tant Rensie. I was staying with cousins in the Free State when it happened. It was on my return to Klipkraal that I first heard of the confusions over her burial. Tant Rensie wanted Sofietjie buried in the garden in front of her house. This was not allowed by the town council. Then Tant Rensie requested that Sofietjie should be buried among white people. The Women's Association and the M.S.A. organised protest meetings, and finally poor Sofietjie was buried in the cemetery just the other side of the coloured location.

Oom Gawie, the town's only taxi driver, took Tant Rensie to Sofietjie's grave whenever her health allowed it. She would sit there for so long – a camp stool went with her every time – that Oom Gawie developed the habit of popping back to town for a quick nip. One day, while he was away, Tant Rensie was caught in a thunderstorm that signalled her end: she developed pneumonia.

Oom Gawie gave up drinking for some time, from remorse, but the sacrifice was uncalled for: Tant Rensie didn't want to live any longer. Everyone said so.

Her will was an odd one. The town inherited her money to build a hospital, but she stipulated one condition: she wanted to be laid to rest next to Sofietjie.

Klipkraal has a beautiful hospital for such a small place. But someone, the missionary says, someone should care for those graves.

Translated by IAN FERGUSON

Her Warrior

✳   ✳   ✳   ✳   ✳

Jonathan Kariara is a Kikuyu from Kenya. He attended the University College of Makerere in
Uganda, where he earned an honors degree in English. Since then he has been on the staff of the East
African Literature Bureau in Nairobi. His most recent book is *The Coming of Power and Other
Studies: Stories from Kenya's History*.

*S*HE WAS A TALL WOMAN with high cheekbones, now more
emphasized than ever by the loss of her molar teeth. Her lips
were finer than most of her tribe's and wore a shut, rather sour
expression. Her eyes seemed to be always fixed on the distance,
as though she didn't "see" or mind the immediate, but dwelt in
the eternal. She was not like other children's grandmothers
we knew, who would spoil their grandchildren and had their
huts "just outside the hedge" of their sons' homesteads. Grandmother lived three hills away, which was inexplicable.

All the other grandmothers had some relationship with their
aging husbands. Some had strange dreams of how their dead
ones had visited them in their dreams, and would repeat their
last night's experience in great detail, time and time again, thus
relieving the monotony of their existence. There was Grandma
Wacu who was always rescuing her husband from toppling into
the fire as he dozed and would scold him with a mighty wrath in

spite of her neighbours' constant protestations that her husband was stone deaf. There were the "Lizards," so called for their day-long basking in the sun. Their life now consisted of following the course of the sun; outside their respective huts in the morning, under the Mukoigo tree at noon, at the back of their huts at sunset, taking in the last rays of the sun. There was Gacucu (Little Grandmother) who after forty years of married life was still having fights with her husband, and indiscriminately would tell her troubles in great detail to us children, to our great joy but so much to the embarrassment of her married daughters.

Grandmother was different. She never mentioned her husband. If ever she heard any of us refer to him she would instantly snort and push away any small object near her with an impatient sweep of her long arm. If any of us dared ask her why she never mentioned him she would instantly lose her temper and like a broody hen ruffling her feathers would rise to gather her few possessions, for a return journey to her hut three miles away. She had been insulted.

On this occasion, though, she had been asked to come, to see him. He was dying. "Tell her she must come," my father had told the man he sent to her. When she arrived she was greatly changed. She who before had walked with such a firm step for her age, who had such a haughty face, was now in a state of nervous excitement. My mother hurried to meet her at the gate as she arrived. "You must see..." "See what?" snapped Grandmother, pushing her aside and confronting my father. "And so I must come, Karanja. So I'm wanted now?" she almost jeered. He, fearing she might say something which would sorrow both for the rest of their lives, left the house immediately and left Mother to face the old woman. "Who wants me here?" she demanded, stamping here and there with a stick like a blind man "looking" for his way. "Who wants me here?" she repeated. We had always enjoyed her tantrums before, we knew they always ended in her either shortening her visit to us, or in a wonderful mood when simply and vividly she would tell us strange stories of her adventures as a girl, before she married. But now it was different, although she was raving, her mind was not on what she was saying, rather she was like a receiver of bad news who puts off the announcement with gibberish. She kept on looking furtively in the direction of his hut, and Mother, guessing what was worrying her, had to break the news she feared. "He is not there. We persuaded him to go to the mission hospital, Mother," she said. For a few seconds the other woman was like somebody choking. She gasped and swayed and would have fallen unconscious had Mother not done what was very unexpected of her. She who always feared the older woman rushed to where she was standing and gripped her by the shoulders, turning Grandmother to face her. Steadily she gazed into Grandmother's face, as though searching for a clue that would thaw the cold resentment the old woman had built up towards her husband. And her eyes also seemed to accuse the older woman, as if saying, "You too were responsible, even to sending him to the mission hospital." The other woman might have understood her for she did not rave now but was leaning on Mother, helplessly. Mother took her into the house.

This is the story as we came to learn later. They married "outside the tribe." That means, she saw her man and decided in her heart to marry him. He saw her heart's decision, and quietly but finally accepted it. Thus they disregarded all the tribal forms of courting and marriage and let it be known they were going to marry. She simply told her parents she was marrying him, so wounding their pride in the implication that they did not count, tribal customs did not count. A girl must not decide for herself finally whom she is going to marry. But she was marrying Wanyoike, the great warrior, so their pride was partly mollified. He on the other hand could have chosen any bride he wanted to marry. He was a war leader, a great but short-lived war leader.

They were not married for long when the Masai declared war

on the Kikuyu. They had cunningly chosen their moment, for the Kikuyus had just been through a period of famine and were rather weakened. Anger that the Masai should so cunningly involve them, when it was usual for them to be the cunning party, gave them greater courage than they normally possessed when fighting the dreaded Maitha.

The war was fought and the Kikuyu were being driven from hill to hill. Wanyoike, one of the Kikuyu leaders, was blind with anger. For days he had fought, never uttering a word, but as the conviction grew that they would lose the battle his anger grew into such a frenzied hatred of the Masai that he would do anything to see them retreat. Next day he did the unexpected, the unprecedented. He gripped the long arm of a Kikuyu warrior who had fallen dead beside him and chopped it off at the shoulder blade. His living hand gripped the dead one and, waving it aloft, he charged into a group of Masai warriors, striking right and left with the dead man's arm. At first they did not understand what was happening, until one after the other they felt the clammy touch of the dead arm. Then they saw. And fear spread among them, a primeval fear of warm blood coming in contact with the disintegrating dead. One after the other they let out a cry, the inhuman cry of a trapped wild animal. It spread like fire with a wind behind it; it echoed in every warrior, Kikuyu or Masai, so that the Kikuyu paused, paralysed with fear, and the Masai, afraid of "evil-let-loose," took to flight. Seeing them flee the Kikuyu fell to, and made history that day for grandmothers to repeat to their grandchildren of the day the Masai were wholly defeated. But it was curious that not one of them mentioned Wanyoike who caused the victory. To them, as to the defeated Masai, it was greatly shocking, therefore taboo, that the living blood in a man should so dare to come into such close contact with the dead.

Wanyoike came back from the war a lonely man. Once the victory was won they were all afraid of him. Deadly afraid. Many of

them said later that they all wanted to be religiously cleansed after that battle, although they should have been singing victori-
ous. They hurried on to their respective huts, who should have
come back one body, united in and drunk with victory.
Wanyoike crept back to his young wife, afraid of himself. So she
took to protecting him, fiercely. "The battle she fought!" the old
women in the village would say. "You did not dare ask her how
the child she was carrying kicked. It was Wanyoike's, so what interest could you have in it? We never knew the little things she
liked during her time of waiting. She was proud and foolish and
had a way of making you look just like a shrivelled leaf floating on
the wind, with a wave of her hand. You did not dare show up at
her house. What do you want? she would demand, sweeping out
like a mad thing, even though you might have been carrying
anointing oil to her. When the child arrived she had no woman
with her. Then they would add with a shudder: "Some people
think he helped her with the birth of the child."

When the child was a few days old Wanyoike killed a fat ram
and invited his relations to come and meet the "new guest" arrived. There was no beer at the feast, for his wife would not agree
to the feasting and said she would rather go through what she
had recently been through than debase herself by asking any of
those women to help her with beer making. So the feast
Wanyoike provided never came to life, for not even birds can
sing on dry throats. The party was rather flagging when she
came out. "You should have seen her fury, that their relations
should come to bless the child! And she would not eat the meat,
would not touch her special portion, but went about like a sheep
suffering from lockjaw. We had all sympathized with her in the
past but now we were not sorry to see that her husband was very
angry with her, and we knew what his anger meant. It was then
that their fights started. She would bow to no man, but would
lift her long strong arms and with fury would strike. He would
get hold of her and shake her until there was no wind in her. And

they are the ones who had walked together in the cool of the evening, as no other woman dare with her husband. Their fights were still and terrible, like quicksands, each keen to destroy the other. Then one day he decided they could not live together and soon after built her a hut where she now lives. He never called her back but something went out of him with her departure. He quickly grew old and started cooking for himself, ay, one of our warriors ended cooking for himself!"

Mother must have succeeded in persuading Grandmother to see her dying husband. "What are we waiting for, then?" we heard her demand of Mother impatiently. Soon they were outside, ready to go to the hospital. But she was not destined to see her husband any more. As they came out at the door my father came in at the gate. Something in his face must have broken the news to the women. Grandmother looked steadily in his face and something, as it were, snapped in the very core of her being. She did not break down in weeping as many women would have done. She simply turned to pick up the little bag she always carried which had fallen when she saw my father. "It is well," she said, "that I did not see him in those ridiculous things they give them to wear at the hospital. I would never have forgiven him if I had seen him in those – those..." She could not continue but walked to the gate. And as she fumbled to open it she was no longer a proud old lady. She was a tottering old woman who would from now on sit outside her hut, looking at the horizon. "She is watching her girlhood dance in the horizon," her neighbours would say if they saw her sitting thus. But most of the time she saw nothing, nothing.

CHARLES MUNGOSHI

The Setting Sun and the Rolling World

❊   ❊   ❊   ❊   ❊

Charles Mungoshi was born in 1947 in Zimbabwe.
He writes novels as well as short stories, and has won
awards in Africa and from PEN for his work. His
most recent book is *The Setting Sun and the Rolling
World*, a selection of his stories.

OLD MUSONI raised his dusty eyes from his hoe and the un-
changing stony earth he had been tilling and peered into the sky.
The white speck whose sound had disturbed his work and
thoughts was far out at the edge of the yellow sky, near the horizon. Then it disappeared quickly over the southern rim of the
sky and he shook his head. He looked to the west. Soon the sun
would go down. He looked over the sunblasted land and saw the
shadows creeping east, clearer and taller with every moment that
the sun shed each of its rays. Unconsciously wishing for rain and
relief, he bent down again to his work and did not see his son,
Nhamo, approaching.

Nhamo crouched in the dust near his father and greeted him.
The old man half raised his back, leaning against his hoe, and
said what had been bothering him all day long.

"You haven't changed your mind?"

"No, father."

There was a moment of silence. Old Musoni scraped earth off his hoe.

"Have you thought about this, son?"

"For weeks, father."

"And you think that's the only way?"

"There is no other way."

The old man felt himself getting angry again. But this would be the last day he would talk to his son. If his son was going away, he must not be angry. It would be equal to a curse. He himself had taken chances before, in his own time, but he felt too much of a father. He had worked and slaved for his family and the land had not betrayed him. He saw nothing now but disaster and death for his son out there in the world. Lions had long since vanished but he knew of worse animals of prey, animals that wore redder claws than the lion's, beasts that would not leave an unprotected homeless boy alone. He thought of the white metal bird and he felt remorse.

"Think again. You will end dead. Think again, of us, of your family. We have a home, poor though it is, but can you think of a day you have gone without?"

"I have thought everything over, father, I am convinced this is the only way out."

"There is no only way out in the world. Except the way of the land, the way of the family."

"The land is overworked and gives nothing now, father. And the family is almost broken up."

The old man got angry. Yes, the land is useless. True, the family tree is uprooted and it dries in the sun. True, many things are happening that haven't happened before, that we did not think would happen, ever. But nothing is more certain to hold you together than the land and a home, a family. And where do you think you are going, a mere beardless kid with the milk not yet dry on your baby nose? What do you think you will do in the great treacherous world where men twice your age have gone and returned with their backs broken – if they returned at all? What do you know of life? What do you know of the false honey bird that leads you the whole day through the forest to a snake's nest? But all he said was: "Look. What have you asked me and I have denied you? What, that I have, have I not given you for the asking?"

"All. You have given me all, father." And here, too, the son felt hampered, patronized, and his pent-up fury rolled through him. It showed on his face but stayed under control. You have given me damn all and nothing. You have sent me to school and told me the importance of education, and now you ask me to throw it on the rubbish heap and scrape for a living on this tired cold shell of the moon. You ask me to forget it and muck around in this slow dance of death with you. I have this one chance of making my own life, once in all eternity, and now you are jealous. You are afraid of your own death. It is, after all, your own death. I shall be around a while yet. I will make my way home if a home is what I need. I am armed more than you think and wiser than you can dream of. But all he said, too, was:

"Really, father, have no fear for me. I will be all right. Give me this chance. Release me from all obligations and pray for me."

There was a spark in the old man's eyes at these words of his son. But just as dust quickly settles over a glittering pebble revealed by the hoe, so a murkiness hid the gleam in the old man's eye. Words are handles made to the smith's fancy and are liable to break under stress. They are too much fat on the hard unbreaking sinews of life.

"Do you know what you are doing, son?"

"Yes."

"Do you know what you will be a day after you leave home?"

"Yes, father."

"A homeless, nameless vagabond living on dust and rat's droppings, living on thank-yous, sleeping up a tree or down a ditch, in the rain, in the sun, in the cold, with nobody to see you, nobody to talk to, nobody at all to tell your dreams to. Do you know what it is to see your hopes come crashing down like an old house out of season and your dreams turning to ash and dung without a tang of salt in your skull? Do you know what it is to live without a single hope of ever seeing good in your own lifetime?" And to himself: Do you know, young bright ambitious son of my loins, the ruins of time and the pains of old age? Do you know how to live beyond a dream, a hope, a faith? Have you seen black despair, my son?

"I know it, father. I know enough to start on. The rest I shall learn as I go on. Maybe I shall learn to come back."

The old man looked at him and felt: Come back where? Nobody comes back to ruins. You will go on, son. Something you don't know will drive you on along deserted plains, past ruins and more ruins, on and on until there is only one ruin left: yourself. You will break down, without tears, son. You are human, too. Listen to the *haya* – the rain bird – and heed its warning of coming storm: plough no more, it says. And what happens if the storm catches you far, far out on the treeless plain? What then, my son?

But he was tired. They had taken over two months discussing all this. Going over the same ground like animals at a drinking place until, like animals, they had driven the water far deep into the stony earth, until they had sapped all the blood out of life and turned it into a grim skeleton, and now they were creating a stampede on the dust, grovelling for water. Mere thoughts. Mere words. And what are words? Trying to grow a fruit tree in the wilderness.

"Go son, with my blessings. I give you nothing. And when you remember what I am saying you will come back. The land is still yours. As long as I am alive you will find a home waiting for you."

"Thank you, father."

"Before you go, see Chiremba. You are going out into the world. You need something to strengthen yourself. Tell him I shall pay him. Have a good journey, son."

"Thank you, father."

Nhamo smiled and felt a great love for his father. But there were things that belonged to his old world that were just lots of humbug on the mind, empty load, useless scrap. He would go to Chiremba but he would burn the charms as soon as he was away from home and its sickening environment. A man stands on his feet and guts. Charms were for you – so was God, though much later. But for us now the world is godless, no charms will work. All that is just the opium you take in the dark in the hope of a light. You don't need that now. You strike a match for a light. Nhamo laughed.

He could be so easily lighthearted. Now his brain worked with a fury only known to visionaries. The psychological ties were now broken, only the biological tied him to his father. He was free. He too remembered the aeroplane which his father had seen just before their talk. Space had no bounds and no ties. Floating laws ruled the darkness and he would float with the fiery balls. He was the sun, burning itself out every second and shedding tons of energy which it held in its power, giving it the thrust to drag its brood wherever it wanted to. This was the law that held him: the mystery that his father and ancestors had failed to grasp and which had caused their being wiped off the face of the earth. This thinking reached such a pitch that he began to sing, imitating as intimately as he could Satchmo's voice: "What a wonderful world." It was Satchmo's voice that he turned to when he felt buoyant.

Old Musoni did not look at his son as he left him. Already, his mind was trying to focus at some point in the dark unforeseeable future. Many things could happen and while he still breathed he would see that nothing terribly painful happened to his family, especially to his stubborn last-born, Nhamo. Tomorrow, before

sunrise, he would go to see Chiremba and ask him to throw
bones over the future of his son. And if there were a couple of ancestors who needed appeasement, he would do it while he was
still around.

He noticed that the sun was going down and he scraped the
earth off his hoe.

The sun was sinking slowly, bloody red, blunting and blur-
ring all the objects that had looked sharp in the light of day. Soon
a chilly wind would blow over the land and the cold cloudless sky
would send down beads of frost like white ants over the unprotected land.

II

The Man with Bulging Pockets

✳   ✳   ✳   ✳   ✳

Toshio Mori was born in Oakland, California, in
1910, and is known as one of the foremost chron-
iclers of the Japanese-American community.

*T*HERE WAS A MAN at Tanforan Assembly Center who was
noted for his bulging pockets and for his admiring following.
From the first day he stepped into the grounds of the former
racetrack he was singled out by the young, and not many days
passed before everyone began to call him "Grandpa." That was
the beginning of his growing fame, perhaps unequaled by anyone at Tanforan with the exception of the most noted thorough-
breds of the prewar days. His smiling old face, wrinkled with
time and energy, bobbed in and out of the children's gathering.
Whenever he went the cries of "Grandpa! Here comes Grandpa!" trailed him, and his smile broadened more than ever.

No one in the community ever saw him before and for a long
while people did not know where he lived. Then one day his
young friends trailed him to his room which he shared with his
wife. Day after day the children came to his door, calling his
name, and when home he would open his door and come out
with a boxful of candies. Children with sharp eyes began to notice his specially made pockets all over his coat and they would
cluster around him with wide-open eyes for surprises and
sweets.

As the people from many communities of the Bay Region entered the gates of the center they soon learned of Grandpa, the man with a houseful of candies and sweets, and his unaccountable amount of cash in the bank. Some of his new acquaintances swore that he was the richest man in Tanforan with hidden treasure in every state of the union, while others claimed that he had retired with several thousand in cash and was using it as "candy money" for the children. When the old folks commended him for his generosity he simply smiled and brushed off the compliment, but when someone in his young following asked him how rich he was, he would give some kind of an answer.

"Yes, Sammy," he would say and nod. "I am rich. I am not rich with money perhaps but I am rich. I am rich for I think I am rich, and I have no aim for money-making now."

But Sammy was still curious. "But if you were poor would you like to be rich with money so you could buy us candy?"

Grandpa would then slap his knees and roar with laughter and nod his head. "Yes, Sammy. Then I would like to be rich with money."

As the number of his friends grew Grandpa found himself short of help and soon the spry Sammy was appointed the head assistant. On Grandpa's daily walk around the center Sammy would accompany him and assist in passing out the sweets. From all barracks the boys and girls would come running with shouts of glee, dropping their toys and playthings. Boys in high spirits would confide in him their hopes and ambitions, making Grandpa smile.

"When I grow big I'll buy tobacco for Grandpa. I'll buy many cans of the best for him," one of the boys would cry.

"Grandpa, we'll all buy tobaccos for you. So many tobaccos that you won't ever have to worry about it," the second boy would exclaim.

"Yes?" Grandpa would ask with a twinkle in his eyes.

"You bet your life," a chorus would reply.

"Thank you, thank you," Grandpa would say and pat the up-lifted heads.

"And when you die, Grandpa, we'll carry your coffin to the grave. We'll remember you, Grandpa. Always," Sammy would exclaim.

Grandpa would chuckle and nod his head in appreciation. "Now I feel safe and comfortable no matter what happens. But if you wish to carry my coffin, you boys must eat and sleep a lot and grow big and strong."

As the center grew in population all sorts of people began to crop out and even Grandpa had his troubles. Out of the thousands of newcomers who had come later, an old bachelor who was once a friend of Grandpa's looked enviously at his popularity. The children called him The Old Man. With shrewd eyes he took to the trails of Grandpa's daily round, seeking a bigger following than Grandpa's and a greater popularity. He soon learned that Grandpa's daily work began at eight in the morning from the west end of the center, so The Old Man set his walking hour half an hour later to undo whatever Grandpa had accomplished for the day.

For a short while Grandpa did not know he had a rival until one day one of his young friends told him about an old man who also came around with candies and sweets.

"Fine, fine! He must be a very nice man," Grandpa heartily cried. "Don't you find his candies good too?"

"Yes, he gives us more than you, Grandpa," one of the boys said.

"Is that so? He must be rich then, both in money and otherwise," Grandpa said.

"I do not like him, Grandpa. He gives us lots of candies but still I do not like him," Sammy said.

Grandpa hushed Sammy so the other children would not hear. "Do not be too hasty, child. He must be nice to be so generous. You must give him time. Try and understand him."

"I still don't like him," Sammy replied.

The Old Man made very little progress with Grandpa's following but he began to look for the children of the newcomers and here he had luck. As time went on his following too became quite large but he was dissatisfied. He wanted Grandpa's following. He wished to be the only popular man of the center and this he earnestly set out to accomplish once and for all.

Grandpa's staunch young followers pleaded with Grandpa about the coming nemesis but he laughed it off.

"He's doing good, boys. He makes people happy. You should not tear down the good he is doing," Grandpa said.

"But he talks bad about you," his young friends cried.

Grandpa would not listen. "That is all talk, children. I would not believe such things until I hear directly from him."

At first Grandpa did not hear The Old Man talk, but one afternoon when he and Sammy were late going on their round he overheard The Old Man's words. The Old Man was talking to the young people.

"Grandpa is a no-good man. Do not accept his candy, boys and girls," The Old Man was saying. "His candies are bad and you musn't touch them. Take mine."

Sammy pulled at Grandpa's sleeve. "Did you hear that, Grandpa? Did you hear The Old Man?"

Grandpa nodded his head quietly and continued walking. For a moment his face became stern and set, and his eyes were glued to the ground. Sammy watched him with concern.

"Don't feel bad, Grandpa. It's all right. We all like you," Sammy cried.

Grandpa patted his head and his familiar smile returned. Several minutes later he was roaring with laughter as he watched the youngsters romp around the playground. His eyes twinkled and his greetings reached the barracks where the children lived and played. His bulging pockets were reached into many times and soon they were emptied, and the youngsters sat around Grandpa munching their sweets and waiting for Grandpa's little stories. Grandpa looked at the gathering and beamed with pleasure. He watched the youngsters' faces whose features were yet unscarred by the wear and tear of life and nodded his head hopefully. He patted their heads and playfully pinched their cheeks. The youngsters noticed his silence and curiously looked at his face.

"What's the matter, Grandpa? What's wrong?" one tiny voice asked.

"Nothing, nothing. Everything is all right. Where the children live there is life. Do you know that, boys and girls? You are very valuable people. We old folks are worthless and some day you are going to take our places," said Grandpa.

The children jumped around happily. Their cries filled the air, and the passersby beamed at the group. Grandpa waved his hands and began his storytelling. The youngsters leaned forward attentively. Suddenly the attention of the group was dispersed by whispers. The Old Man was coming up the road.

Grandpa hailed The Old Man but the latter walked by silently. He had two handfuls of candies, smiling at the children. Several of the youngsters ran after him, following him as he showered them with packages of gum and chocolate bars. The rest of the children watched hesitantly and then they saw Sammy sit down and lean closer to Grandpa to hear the story. The children followed suit and Grandpa looked at his crowd happily and smiled. He chuckled loudly and his little friends joined him.

"What is so funny, Grandpa?" Sammy asked innocently. "Aren't you mad at The Old Man?"

Grandpa shook his head and smiled. "I am not mad because I have many nice friends too. He needs nice little friends, too, don't you think?"

The group remained silent, and Grandpa picked up his story. As he watched the rapt features of his little friends his face became lined with concern. In that moment of a dark recess a foreboding thought flashed in his mind. The Old Man and he belonged to one big circle where no ill feelings and furtive deeds need enter. They should join hands and rejoice in the heart of a child. They should inspire and sing in the oneness of hope, but no. They were partisans, and the split in their circle was the enigma and blot of all mankind.

Humaweepi, the Warrior Priest

✳   ✳   ✳   ✳   ✳

Leslie Marmon Silko is a member of the Laguna
Pueblo tribe, and has written several books, including *Ceremony*, *Storyteller*, and, as co-author
with James Wright, *The Delicacy and
Strength of Lace*.

*T*HE OLD MAN didn't really teach him much; mostly they just lived. Occasionally Humaweepi would meet friends his own age who still lived with their families in the pueblo, and they would ask him what he was doing; they seemed disappointed when he told them.

"That's nothing," they would say.

Once this had made Humaweepi sad and his uncle noticed. "Oh," he said when Humaweepi told him, "that shows you how little they know."

They returned to the pueblo for the ceremonials and special days. His uncle stayed in the kiva with the other priests, and Humaweepi usually stayed with clan members because his mother and father had been very old when he was born and now they were gone. Sometimes during these stays, when the pueblo was full of the activity and excitement of the dances or the fiesta when the Christians paraded out of the pueblo church carrying the saint, Humaweepi would wonder why he was living out in the hills with the old man. When he was twelve he thought he had it all figured out: the old man just wanted someone to live with him and help him with the goat and to chop wood and carry water. But it was peaceful in this place, and Humaweepi discovered that after all these years of sitting beside his uncle in the evenings, he knew the songs and chants for all the seasons, and he was beginning to learn the prayers for the trees and plants and animals. "Oh," Humaweepi said to himself, "I have been learning all this time and I didn't even know it."

Once the old man told Humaweepi to prepare for a long trip.

"Overnight?"

The old man nodded.

So Humaweepi got out a white cotton sack and started filling it with jerked venison, piki bread, and dried apples. But the old man shook his head sternly. It was late June then, so Humaweepi didn't bother to bring the blankets; he had learned to sleep on the ground like the old man did.

"Human beings are special," his uncle had told him once, "which means they can do anything. They can sleep on the ground like the doe and fawn."

And so Humaweepi had learned how to find the places in the scrub-oak thickets where the deer had slept, where the dry oak leaves were arranged into nests. This is where he and his uncle slept, even in the autumn when the nights were cold and Humaweepi could hear the leaves snap in the middle of the night and drift to the ground.

Sometimes they carried food from home, but often they went without food or blankets. When Humaweepi asked him what they would eat, the old man had waved his hand at the sky and earth around them. "I am a human being, Humaweepi," he said; "I eat anything." On these trips they had gathered grass roots and washed them in little sandstone basins made by the wind to catch rain water. The roots had a rich, mealy taste. Then they left the desert below and climbed into the mesa country, and the old man had led Humaweepi to green leafy vines hanging from crevasses in the face of the sandstone cliffs. "Wild grapes," he said as he dropped some tiny dark-purple berries into Humaweepi's open palms. And in the high mountains there were wild iris roots and the bulbs from wild tulips which grew among the lacy ferns and green grass beside the mountain streams. They had gone out like this in each season. Summer and fall, and finally, spring and winter. "Winter isn't easy," the old man had said. "All the animals are hungry—not just you."

So this time, when his uncle shook his head at the food, Humaweepi left it behind as he had many times before. His uncle took the special leather pouch off the nail on the wall, and Humaweepi pulled his own buckskin bundle out from under his mattress. Inside he had a few objects of his own. A dried blossom. Fragile and yellow. A smooth pink quartz crystal in the shape of a star. Tiny turquoise beads the color of a summer sky. And a black obsidian arrowhead, shiny and sharp. They each had special meaning to him, and the old man had instructed him to assemble these things with special meaning. "Someday maybe you will derive strength from these things." That's what the old man had said.

They walked west toward the distant blue images of the mountain peaks. The water in the Rio Grande was still cold. Humaweepi was aware of the dampness on his feet: when he got back from his journey he decided he would make sandals for himself because it took hours for his boots to dry out again. His uncle wore old sandals woven from twisted yucca fiber and they dried out almost immediately. The old man didn't approve of boots and shoes—bad for you, he said. In the winter he wore buckskin moccasins and in the warm months, these yucca sandals.

They walked all day, steadily, stopping occasionally when the old man found a flower or herb or stone that he wanted Humaweepi to see. And it seemed to Humaweepi that he had learned the names of everything, and he said so to his uncle.

The old man frowned and poked at a small blue flower with his walking stick. "That's what a priest must know," he said and walked rapidly then, pointing at stones and shrubs. "How old are you?" he demanded.

"Nineteen," Humaweepi answered.

"All your life," he said, "every day, I have been teaching you."

After that they walked along in silence, and Humaweepi began to feel anxious; all of a sudden he knew that something was going to happen on this journey. That night they reached the white sandstone cliffs at the foot of the mountain foothills. At the base of these cliffs were shallow overhangs with sandy floors. They slept in the sand under the rock overhang; in the night Humaweepi woke up to the call of a young owl; the sky was bright with stars and a half-moon. The smell of the night air made him shiver and he buried himself more deeply in the cliff sand.

In the morning they gathered tumbleweed sprouts that were succulent and tender. As they climbed the cliffs there were wild grapevines, and under the fallen leaves around the vine roots, the old man uncovered dried grapes shrunken into tiny sweet raisins. By noon they had reached the first of the mountain streams. There they washed and drank water and rested.

The old man frowned and pointed at Humaweepi's boots. "Take them off," he told Humaweepi; "leave them here until we come back."

So Humaweepi pulled off his cowboy boots and put them under a lichen-covered boulder near a big oak tree where he could find them. Then Humaweepi relaxed, feeling the coolness of air on his bare feet. He watched his uncle, dozing in the sun with his back against a big pine. The old man's hair had been white and long ever since Humaweepi could remember; but the old face was changing, and Humaweepi could see the weariness there – a weariness not from their little journey but from a much longer time in this world. Someday he will die, Humaweepi was thinking. He will be gone and I will be by myself. I will have to do the things he did. I will have to take care of things.

Humaweepi had never seen the lake before. It appeared suddenly as they reached the top of a hill covered with aspen trees. Humaweepi looked at his uncle and was going to ask him about the lake, but the old man was singing and feeding corn pollen from his leather pouch to the mountain winds. Humaweepi stared at the lake and listened to the songs. The songs were snowstorms with sounds as soft and cold as snowflakes; the songs were spring rain and wild ducks returning. Humaweepi could hear this; he could hear his uncle's voice become the night wind – high-pitched and whining in the trees. Time was lost and there was only the space, the depth, the distance of the lake surrounded by the mountain peaks.

When Humaweepi looked up from the lake he noticed that the sun had moved down into the western part of the sky. He looked around to find his uncle. The old man was below him, kneeling on the edge of the lake, touching a big gray boulder and singing softly. Humaweepi made his way down the narrow rocky trail to the edge of the lake. The water was crystal and clear like air; Humaweepi could see the golden rainbow colors of the trout that lived there. Finally the old man motioned for Humaweepi to come to him. He pointed at the gray boulder that lay half in the lake and half on the shore. It was then that Humaweepi saw what it was. The bear. Magic creature of the mountains, powerful ally to men. Humaweepi unrolled his buckskin bundle and picked up the tiny beads – sky-blue turquoise and coral that was dark red. He sang the bear song and stepped into the icy, clear water to lay the beads on bear's head, gray granite rock, resting above the lake, facing west.

> *"Bear*
> *resting in the mountains*
> *sleeping by the lake*
> *Bear*
> *I come to you, a man,*
> *to ask you:*
> *Stand beside us in our battles*
> *walk with us in peace.*
> *Bear*
> *I ask you for your power*
> *I am the warrior priest.*
> *I ask you for your power*
> *I am the warrior priest."*

It wasn't until he had finished singing the song that Humaweepi realized what the words said. He turned his head toward the old man. He smiled at Humaweepi and nodded his head. Humaweepi nodded back.

HUMAWEEPI AND HIS FRIEND were silent for a long time. Finally Humaweepi said, "I'll tell you what my uncle told me, one winter, before he left. We took a trip to the mountain. It was early January, but the sun was warm and down here the snow was gone. We left early in the morning when the sky in the east was dark gray and the brightest star was still shining low in the western sky. I remember he didn't wear his ceremonial moccasins; he wore his old yucca sandals. I asked him about that.

"He said, 'Oh, you know the badger and the squirrel. Same shoes summer and winter,' but I think he was making that up, because when we got to the sandstone cliffs he buried the sandals in the sandy bottom of the cave where we slept and after that he walked on bare feet – up the cliff and along the mountain trail.

"There was snow on the shady side of the trees and big rocks, but the path we followed was in the sun and it was dry. I could hear melting snow – the icy water trickling down into the little streams and the little streams flowing into the big stream in the canyon where yellow bee flowers grow all summer. The sun felt warm on my body, touching me, but my breath still made steam in the cold mountain air.

"'Aren't your feet cold?' I asked him.

"He stopped and looked at me for a long time, then shook his head. 'Look at these old feet,' he said. 'Do you see any corns or bunions?'

"I shook my head.

"'That's right,' he said, 'my feet are beautiful. No one has feet like these. Especially you people who wear shoes and boots.' He walked on ahead before he said anything else. 'You have seen babies, haven't you?' he asked.

"I nodded, but I was wondering what this had to do with the old man's feet.

"'Well, then you've noticed their grandmothers and their mothers, always worried about keeping the feet warm. But have you watched the babies? Do they care? No!' the old man said triumphantly, 'they do not care. They play outside on a cold winter day, no shoes, no jacket, because they aren't cold.' He hiked on, moving rapidly, excited by his own words; then he stopped at the stream. 'But human beings are what they are. It's not long before they are taught to be cold and they cry for their shoes.'

"The old man started digging around the edge of a stream, using a crooked, dry branch to poke through the melting snow. 'Here,' he said as he gave me a fat, round root, 'try this.'

"I squatted at the edge of the rushing, swirling water, full of mountain dirt, churning, swelling, and rolling – rich and brown and muddy with ice pieces flashing in the sun. I held the root motionless under the force of the stream water; the ice coldness of the water felt pure and clear as the ice that clung to the rocks in midstream. When I pulled my hand back it was stiff. I shook it and the root and lifted them high toward the sky.

"The old man laughed, and his mouth was full of the milky fibers of the root. He walked up the hill, away from the sound of the muddy stream surging through the snowbanks. At the top of the hill there was a grove of big aspens; it was colder, and the snow hadn't melted much.

"'Your feet,' I said to him. 'They'll freeze.'

"The snow was up to my ankles now. He was sitting on a fallen aspen, with his feet stretched out in front of him and his eyes half closed, facing into the sun.

"'Does the wolf freeze his feet?' the old man asked me.

"I shook my head.

"'Well then,' he said.

"'But aren't you a wolf,' I started to say.

"The old man's eyes opened wide and then looked at me narrowly, sharply, squinting and shining. He gave a long, wailing, wolf cry with his head raised toward the winter sky.

"It was all white – pale white – the sky, the aspens bare white, smooth and white as the snow frozen on the ground. The wolf cry echoed off the rocky mountain slopes around us; in the distance I thought I heard a wailing answer."

A L I C E   W A L K E R

To Hell with Dying

✳   ✳   ✳   ✳   ✳

Alice Walker won a Pulitzer Prize and an American
Book Award for her novel *The Color Purple*. She has
published novels, children's literature, poetry, a bi-
ography of Langston Hughes, and a Zora Neale
Hurston reader. Her most recent book is
The Temple of My Familiar.

*M*R. SWEET was a diabetic and an alcoholic and a guitar
player and lived down the road from us on a neglected cotton
farm. My older brothers and sisters got the most benefit from
Mr. Sweet, for when they were growing up he had quite a few
years ahead of him and so was capable of being called back from
the brink of death any number of times – whenever the voice of
my father reached him as he lay expiring. "To hell with dying,
man," my father would say, pushing the wife away from the bedside (in tears although she knew the death was not necessarily the
last one unless Mr. Sweet really wanted it to be). "These children want Mr. Sweet!" And they did want him, for at a signal
from Father they would come crowding around the bed and
throw themselves on the covers, and whoever was the smallest at
the time would kiss him all over his wrinkled brown face and begin to tickle him so that he would laugh all down in his stomach,
and his mustache, which was long and sort of straggly, would
shake like Spanish moss and was also that color.

Mr. Sweet had been ambitious as a boy, wanted to be a doctor or lawyer or sailor, only to find that black men fare better if they are not. Since he could become none of these things he turned to fishing as his one earnest career and playing the guitar as his sole claim to doing anything extraordinarily well. His son, the only one that he and his wife, Miss Mary, had, was shiftless as the day is long and spent money as if he were trying to see the bottom of the mint, which Mr. Sweet would tell him was the clean brown palm of his hand. Miss Mary loved her "baby," however, and worked hard to get him the "li'l necessaries" of life, which turned out mostly to be women.

Mr. Sweet was a tall, thinnish man with thick kinky hair going dead white. He was dark brown, his eyes were very squinty and sort of bluish, and he chewed Brown Mule tobacco. He was constantly on the verge of being blind drunk, for he brewed his own liquor and was not in the least a stingy sort of man, and was always very melancholy and sad, though frequently when he was "feelin' good" he'd dance around the yard with us, usually keeling over just as my mother came to see what the commotion was.

Toward all of us children he was very kind, and had the grace to be shy with us, which is unusual in grown-ups. He had great respect for my mother for she never held his drunkenness against him and would let us play with him even when he was about to fall in the fireplace from drink. Although Mr. Sweet would sometimes lose complete or nearly complete control of his head and neck so that he would loll in his chair, his mind remained strangely acute and his speech not too affected. His ability to be drunk and sober at the same time made him an ideal playmate, for he was as weak as we were and we could usually best him in wrestling, all the while keeping a fairly coherent conversation going.

We never felt anything of Mr. Sweet's age when we played with him. We loved his wrinkles and would draw some on our brows to be like him, and his white hair was my special treasure and he knew it and would never come to visit us just after he had had his hair cut off at the barbershop. Once he came to our house for something, probably to see my father about fertilizer for his crops because, although he never paid the slightest attention to his crops, he liked to know what things would be best to use on them if he ever did. Anyhow, he had not come with his hair since he had just had it shaved off at the barbershop. He wore a huge straw hat to keep off the sun and also to keep his head away from me. But as soon as I saw him I ran up and demanded that he take me up and kiss me with his funny mustache, which smelled so strongly of tobacco. Looking forward to burying my small fingers into his woolly hair I threw away his hat only to find he had done something to his hair, that it was no longer there! I let out a squall which made my mother think that Mr. Sweet had finally dropped me in the well or something and from that day I've been wary of men in hats. However, not long after, Mr. Sweet showed up with his hair grown out and just as white and kinky and impenetrable as it ever was.

Mr. Sweet used to call me his princess, and I believed it. He made me feel pretty at five and six, and simply outrageously devastating at the blazing age of eight and a half. When he came to our house with his guitar the whole family would stop whatever they were doing and sit around him and listen to him play. He liked to play "Sweet Georgia Brown," that was what he called me sometimes, and also he liked to play "Caldonia" and all sorts of sweet, sad, wonderful songs which he sometimes made up. It was from one of these songs that I learned that he had had to marry Miss Mary when he had in fact loved somebody else (now living in Chi-ca-go, or De-stroy, Michigan). He was not sure that Joe Lee, her "baby," was also his baby. Sometimes he would cry and that was an indication that he was about to die again. And so we would all get prepared, for we were sure to be called upon.

I was seven the first time I remember actually participating in

one of Mr. Sweet's "revivals" – my parents told me I had partici-
pated before, I had been the one chosen to kiss him and tickle
him long before I knew the rite of Mr. Sweet's rehabilitation. He
had come to our house, it was a few years after his wife's death,
and was very sad, and also, typically, very drunk. He sat on the
floor next to me and my older brother; the rest of the children
were grown up and lived elsewhere, and began to play his guitar
and cry. I held his woolly head in my arms and wished I could
have been old enough to have been the woman he loved so much
and that I had not been lost years and years ago.

When he was leaving, my mother said to us that we'd better
sleep light that night for we'd probably have to go over to Mr.
Sweet's before daylight. And we did. For soon after we had gone
to bed one of the neighbors knocked on our door and called my
father and said that Mr. Sweet was sinking fast and if he wanted
to get in a word before the crossover he'd better shake a leg and
get over to Mr. Sweet's house. All the neighbors knew to come to
our house if something was wrong with Mr. Sweet, but they did
not know how we always managed to make him well, or at least
stop him from dying, when he was often so near death. As soon
as we heard the cry we got up, my brother and I and my mother
and father, and put on our clothes. We hurried out of the house
and down the road, for we were always afraid that we might
someday be too late and Mr. Sweet would get tired of dallying.

When we got to the house, a very poor shack really, we found
the front room full of neighbors and relatives and a man met us at
the door and said that it was all very sad that old Mr. Sweet Little
(for Little was his family name, although we mostly ignored it)
was about to kick the bucket. He advised my parents not to take
my brother and me into the "death room," seeing we were so
young and all, but we were so much more accustomed to the
death room than he that we ignored him and dashed in without
giving his warning a second thought. I was almost in tears, for
these deaths upset me fearfully, and the thought of how much

depended on me and my brother (who was such a ham most of the time) made me very nervous.

The doctor was bending over the bed and turned back to tell us for at least the tenth time in the history of my family that, alas, old Mr. Sweet Little was dying and that the children had best not see the face of implacable death (I didn't know what "implacable" was, but whatever it was, Mr. Sweet was not!). My father pushed him rather abruptly out of the way saying, as he always did and very loudly, for he was saying it to Mr. Sweet, "To hell with dying, man, these children want Mr. Sweet" – which was my cue to throw myself upon the bed and kiss Mr. Sweet all around the whiskers and under the eyes and around the collar of his nightshirt where he smelled so strongly of all sorts of things, mostly liniment.

I was very good at bringing him around, for as soon as I saw that he was struggling to open his eyes I knew he was going to be all right, and so could finish my revival sure of success. As soon as his eyes were open he would begin to smile and that way I knew that I had surely won. Once, though, I got a tremendous scare, for he could not open his eyes and later I learned that he had had a stroke and that one side of his face was stiff and hard to get into motion. When he began to smile I could tickle him in earnest because I was sure that nothing would get in the way of his laughter, although once he began to cough so hard that he almost threw me off his stomach, but that was when I was very small, little more than a baby, and my bushy hair had gotten in his nose.

When we were sure he would listen to us we would ask him why he was in bed and when he was coming to see us again and could we play with his guitar, which more than likely would be leaning against the bed. His eyes would get all misty and he would sometimes cry out loud, but we never let it embarrass us, for he knew that we loved him and that we sometimes cried too for no reason. My parents would leave the room to just the three of us; Mr. Sweet, by that time, would be propped up in bed with a number of pillows behind his head and with me sitting and lying on his shoulder and along his chest. Even when he had trouble breathing he would not ask me to get down. Looking into my eyes he would shake his white head and run a scratchy old finger all around my hairline, which was rather low down, nearly to my eyebrows, and made some people say I looked like a baby monkey.

My brother was very generous in all this, he let me do all the revivaling – he had done it for years before I was born and so was glad to be able to pass it on to someone new. What he would do while I talked to Mr. Sweet was pretend to play the guitar, in fact pretend that he was a young version of Mr. Sweet, and it always made Mr. Sweet glad to think that someone wanted to be like him – of course, we did not know this then, we played the thing by ear, and whatever he seemed to like, we did. We were desperately afraid that he was just going to take off one day and leave us.

It did not occur to us that we were doing anything special; we had not learned that death was final when it did come. We thought nothing of triumphing over it so many times, and in fact became a trifle contemptuous of people who let themselves be carried away. It did not occur to us that if our own father had been dying we could not have stopped it, that Mr. Sweet was the only person over whom we had power.

When Mr. Sweet was in his eighties I was studying in the university many miles from home. I saw him whenever I went home, but he was never on the verge of dying that I could tell and I began to feel that my anxiety for his health and psychological well-being was unnecessary. By this time he not only had a mustache but was beginning to grow a beard. He was very peaceful, fragile, gentle, and the only jarring note about him was his old guitar, which he still played in the old sad, sweet, down-home blues way.

On Mr. Sweet's ninetieth birthday I was finishing my doctorate in Massachusetts and had been making arrangements to go home for several weeks' rest. That morning I got a telegram telling me that Mr. Sweet was dying again and could I please drop everything and come home. Of course I could. My dissertation could wait and my teachers would understand when I explained to them after I got back. I ran to the phone, called the airport, and within four hours I was speeding along the dusty road to Mr. Sweet's.

The house was more dilapidated than when I was last there, but it was overgrown with yellow roses which my family had planted many years ago. The air was heavy and sweet and very peaceful. I felt strange walking through the gate and up the old rickety steps. But the strangeness left me as I caught sight of the thin body I loved so well beneath the familiar quilt coverlet. Mr. Sweet!

His eyes were closed tight and his hands, crossed over his stomach, were thin and delicate, no longer scratchy. I remembered how as a small child I had run and jumped up on him just anywhere; now I knew he would not be able to support my weight. I looked around at my parents, and was surprised to see that my father and mother also looked old and frail. My father, his own hair very gray, leaned over the quietly sleeping old man, who, incidentally, smelled still of wine and tobacco, and said, as he'd done so many times, "To hell with dying, man! My daughter is home to see Mr. Sweet!" My brother hadn't been able to come, as he was in the war in Asia. I bent down and gently stroked the closed eyes and gradually they began to open. The closed, wine-stained lips twitched a little, then parted in a warm, slightly embarrassed smile. Mr. Sweet could see me and he recognized me and his eyes looked very spry and twinkly for a moment. I put my head down on the pillow next to his and we just looked at each other for a long time. Then he began to trace my peculiar hairline with a thin, smooth finger. I closed my eyes when his finger halted above my ear (he used to rejoice at the dirt in my ears when I was little), his hand stayed cupped around my cheek. When I opened my eyes, sure that I had reached him in time, his were closed.

Even at twenty-four how could I believe that I had failed? that Mr. Sweet was really gone? He had never gone before. But when I looked up at my parents I saw that they were holding back tears. They had loved him dearly. He was like a piece of rare and delicate china which was always being saved from breaking and which finally fell. I looked long at the old face, the wrinkled forehead, the red lips, the hands that still reached out to me. Soon I felt my father pushing something cool into my hands. It was Mr. Sweet's guitar. He had asked him months before to give it to me; he had known that even if I came next time he would not be able to respond in the old way. He did not want me to feel that my trip had been for nothing.

The old guitar! I plucked the strings, hummed "Sweet Georgia Brown." The magic of Mr. Sweet lingered still in the smooth wooden box. Through the window I could catch the fragrant delicate scent of tender yellow roses. The man on the high old-fashioned bed with the quilt coverlet and the glowing white hair had been my first love.

III

RUTH PRAWER JHABVALA

The Man with the Dog

✳   ✳   ✳   ✳   ✳

Ruth Prawer Jhabvala was born in Germany of
Polish-Jewish parents, educated in England, and
married to an Indian architect. She and her husband
lived in Delhi from 1951 to 1975, and since then
have divided their time between Delhi and New
York. She has published nine novels and several
collections of short stories.

I THINK OF MYSELF sometimes as I was in the early days,
and I see myself moving around my husband's house the way I
used to do: freshly bathed, flowers in my hair, I go from room to
room and look in corners to see that everything is clean. I walk
proudly. I know myself to be loved and respected as one who
faithfully fulfills all her duties in life – toward God, parents, husband, children, servants, and the poor. When I pass the prayer
room, I join my hands and bow my head and sweet reverence
flows in me from top to toe. I know my prayers to be pleasing and
acceptable.

Perhaps it is because they remember me as I was in those days
that my children get so angry with me every time they see me
now. They are all grown up now and scattered in many parts of
India. When they need me, or when my longing for them becomes too strong, I go and visit one or other of them. What happiness! They crowd round me, I kiss them and hug them and

cry, I laugh with joy at everything my little grandchildren say and do, we talk all night there is so much to tell. As the days pass, however, we touch on other topics that are not so pleasant, or even if we don't touch on them, they are there and we think of them, and our happiness becomes clouded. I feel guilty and, worse, I begin to feel restless, and the more restless I am the more guilty I feel. I want to go home, though I dare not admit it to them. At the same time I want to stay, I don't ever ever want to leave them – my darling beloved children and grandchildren for whom what happiness it would be to lay down my life! But I have to go, the restlessness is burning me up, and I begin to tell them lies. I say that some urgent matter has come up and I have to consult my lawyer. Of course, they know it is lies, and they argue with me and quarrel and say things that children should not have to say to their mother; so that when at last I have my way and my bags are packed, our grief is more than only that of parting. All the way home, tears stream down my cheeks and my feelings are in turmoil, as the train carries me farther and farther away from them, although it is carrying me toward that which I have been hungering and burning for all the time I was with them.

Yes, I, an old woman, a grandmother many times over – I hunger and burn! And for whom? For an old man. And having said that, I feel like throwing my hands before my face and laughing out loud, although of course it may happen, as it often does to me nowadays, that my laughter will change into sobs and then back again as I think of him, of that old man whom I love so much. And how he would hate it, to be called an old man! Again I laugh when I think of his face if he could hear me call him that. The furthest he has got is to think of himself as middle-aged. Only the other day I heard him say to one of his lady friends, "Yes, now that we're all middle-aged, we have to take things a bit more slowly"; and he stroked his hand over his hair, which he combs very carefully so that the bald patches don't show, and looked sad because he was middle-aged.

I think of the first time I ever saw him. I remember everything exactly. I had been to Spitzer's to buy some little Swiss cakes, and Ram Lal, who was already my chauffeur in those days, had started the car and was just taking it out of its parking space when he drove straight into the rear bumper of a car that was backing into the adjacent space. This car was not very grand, but the Sahib who got out of it was. He wore a beautifully tailored suit with creases in the trousers and a silk tie and a hat on his head; under his arm he carried a very hairy little dog, which was barking furiously. The Sahib too was barking furiously, his face had gone red all over and he shouted abuses at Ram Lal in English. He didn't see me for a while, but when he did he suddenly stopped shouting, almost in the middle of a word. He looked at me as I sat in the back of the Packard in my turquoise sari and a cape made out of an embroidered Kashmiri shawl; even the dog stopped barking. I knew that look well. It was one that men had given me from the time I was fifteen right till—yes, even till I was over forty. It was a look that always filled me with annoyance but also (now that I am so old I can admit it) pride and pleasure. Then, a few seconds later, still looking at me in the same way but by this time with a little smile as well, he raised his hat to me; his hair was blond and thin. I inclined my head, settled my cape around my shoulders, and told Ram Lal to drive on.

In those days I was very pleasure-loving. Children were all quite big, three of them were already in college and the two younger ones at their boarding schools. When they were small and my dear husband was still with us, we lived mostly in the hills or on our estate near X (which now belongs to my eldest son, Shammi); these were quiet, dull places where my dear husband could do all his reading, invite his friends, and listen to music. Our town house was let out in those years, and when we came to see his lawyer or consult some special doctor, we had to stay in a hotel. But after I was left alone and the children were bigger, I kept the town house for myself, because I liked living in town best. I spent a lot of time shopping and bought many costly saris that I did not need; at least twice a week I visited a cinema and I even learned to play cards! I was invited to many tea parties, dinners, and other functions.

It was at one of these that I met him again. We recognized each other at once, and he looked at me in the same way as before, and soon we were making conversation. Now that we are what we are to each other and have been so for all these years, it is difficult for me to look back and see him as I did at the beginning – as a stranger with a stranger's face and a stranger's name. What interested me in him the most at the beginning was, I think, that he was a foreigner; at the time I hadn't met many foreigners, and I was fascinated by so many things about him that seemed strange and wonderful to me. I liked the elegant way he dressed, and the lively way in which he spoke, and his thin fair hair, and the way his face would go red. I was also fascinated by the way he talked to me and to the other ladies: so different from our Indian men who are always a little shy with us and clumsy, and even if they like to talk with us, they don't want anyone to see that they like it. But he didn't care who saw – he would sit on a little stool by the side of the lady with whom he was talking, and he would look up at her and smile and make conversation in a very lively manner, and sometimes, in talking, he would lay his hand on her arm. He was also extra polite with us, he drew back the chair for us when we wanted to sit down or get up, and he would open the door for us, and he lit the cigarettes of those ladies who smoked, and all sorts of other little services that our Indian men would be ashamed of and think beneath their dignity. But the way he did it all, it was full of dignity. And one other thing, when he greeted a lady and wanted her to know that he thought highly of her, he would kiss her hand, and this too was beautiful, although the first time he did it to me I had a shock like electricity going down my spine and I wanted to snatch away my hand from him and wipe it clean on my sari. But afterward I got used to it and I liked it.

His name is Boekelman, he is a Dutchman, and when I first met him he had already been in India for many years. He had come out to do business here, in ivory, and was caught by the war and couldn't get back; and when the war was over, he no longer wanted to go back. He did not earn a big fortune, but it was enough for him. He lived in a hotel suite that he had furnished with his own carpets and pictures, he ate well, he drank well, he had his circle of friends, and a little hairy dog called Susi. At home in Holland all he had left were two aunts and a wife, from whom he was divorced and whom he did not even like to think about (her name was Annemarie, but he always spoke of her as "Once bitten, twice shy"). So India was home for him, although he had not learned any Hindi except *achchha*, which means all right and *pani*, which means water, and he did not know any Indians. All his friends were foreigners; his lady friends also.

Many things have changed now from what they were when I first knew him. He no longer opens the door for me to go in or out, nor does he kiss my hand; he still does it for other ladies, but no longer for me. That's all right, I don't want it, it is not needed. We live in the same house now, for he has given up his hotel room and has moved into a suite of rooms in my house. He pays rent for this, which I don't want but can't refuse, because he insists; and anyway, perhaps it doesn't matter, because it isn't very much money (he has calculated the rent not on the basis of what would have to be paid today but on what it was worth when the house was first built, almost forty years ago). In return, he wishes to have those rooms kept quite separate and that everyone should knock before they go in; he also sometimes gives parties in there for his European friends, to which he may or may not invite me. If he invites me, he will do it like this: "One or two people are dropping in this evening, I wonder if you would care to join us?" Of course I have known long before this about the party, because he has told the cook to get something ready, and the cook has come to me to ask what should be made, and I have given full instructions; if something very special is needed, I make it myself. After he has invited me and I have accepted, the next thing he asks me, "What will you wear?" and he looks at me very critically. He always says women must be elegant, and that was why he first liked me, because in those days I was very careful about my appearance, I bought many new saris and had blouses made to match them, and I went to a beauty parlor and had facial massage and other things. But now all that has vanished, I no longer care about what I look like.

It is strange how often in one lifetime one changes and changes again, even an ordinary person like myself. When I look back, I see myself first as the young girl in my father's house, impatient, waiting for things to happen; then as the calm wife and mother, fulfilling all my many duties; and then again, when children are bigger and my dear husband, many years older than myself, has moved far away from me and I am more his daughter than his wife – then again I am different. In those years we mostly lived in the hills, and I would go for long walks by myself, for hours and hours, sometimes with great happiness to be there among those great green mountains in sun and mist. But sometimes also I was full of misery and longed for something as great and beautiful as those mountains to fill my own life, which seemed, in those years, very empty. But when my dear husband left us forever, I came down from the mountains and then began that fashionable town-life of which I have already spoken. But that too has finished. Now I get up in the mornings, I drink my tea, I walk around the garden with a peaceful heart; I pick a handful of blossoms; and these I lay at the feet of Vishnu in my prayer room. Without taking my bath or changing out of the old cotton sari in which I have spent the night, I sit for many hours on the veranda, doing nothing, only looking out at the flowers and the birds. My thoughts come and go.

At about twelve o'clock Boekelman is ready and comes out of his room. He always likes to sleep late, and after that it always takes him at least one or two hours to get ready. His face is pink and shaved, his clothes are freshly pressed, he smells of shaving lotion and eau de cologne and all the other things he applies out of the rows of bottles on his bathroom shelf. In one hand he has his rolled English umbrella, with the other he holds Susi on a red-leather lead. He is ready to go out. He looks at me, and I can see he is annoyed at the way I am sitting there, rumpled and unbathed. If he is not in a hurry to go, he may stop and talk with me for a while, usually to complain about something; he is never in a very good mood at this time of day. Sometimes he will say the washerman did not press his shirts well, another time that his coffee this morning was stone cold; or he could not sleep all night because of noise coming from the servant quarters; or that a telephone message was not delivered to him promptly enough, or that it looked as if someone had tampered with his mail. I answer him shortly, or sometimes not at all, only go on looking out into the garden; and this always makes him angry, his face becomes very red and his voice begins to shake a little though he tries to control it: "Surely it is not too much to ask," he says, "to have such messages delivered to me clearly and at the right time?" As he speaks, he stabs tiny holes into the ground with his umbrella to emphasize what he is saying. I watch him doing this, and then I say, "Don't ruin my garden." He stares at me in surprise for a moment, after which he deliberately makes another hole with his umbrella and goes on talking: "It so happened it was an extremely urgent message–" I don't let him get far. I'm out of my chair and I shout at him, "You are ruining my garden," and then I go on shouting about other things, and I advance toward him and he begins to retreat backward. "This is ridiculous," he says, and some other things as well, but he can't be heard because I am shouting so loud and the dog too has begun to bark. He walks faster now in order to get out of the gate more quickly, pulling the dog along with him; I follow them, I'm very excited by this time and no longer know what I'm saying. The gardener, who is cutting the hedge, pretends not to hear or see anything but concentrates on his work. At last he is out in the street with the dog, and they walk down it very fast, with the dog turning around to bark and he pulling it along, while I stand at the gate and pursue them with my angry shouts till they have disappeared from sight.

That is the end of my peace and contemplation. Now I am very upset, I walk up and down the garden and through the house, talking to myself and sometimes striking my two fists together. I think bad things about him and talk to him in my thoughts, and likewise in my thoughts he is answering me and these answers make me even more angry. If some servant comes and speaks to me at this time, I get angry with him too and shout so loud that he runs away, and the whole house is very quiet and everyone keeps out of my way. But slowly my feelings begin to change. My anger burns itself out, and I am left with the ashes of remorse. I remember all my promises to myself, all my resolutions never to give way to my bad temper again; I remember my beautiful morning hours, when I felt so full of peace, so close to the birds and trees and sunlight and other innocent things. And with that memory tears spring into my eyes, and I lie down sorrowfully on my bed. Lakshmi, my old woman servant who has been with me nearly forty years, comes in with a cup of tea for me. I sit up and drink it, the tears still on my face and more tears rolling down into my cup. Lakshmi begins to smooth my hair, which has come undone in the excitement, and while she is doing this I talk to her in broken words about my own folly and bad character. She clicks her tongue, contradicts me, praises me, and that makes me suddenly angry again, so that I snatch the comb out of her hand, I throw it against the wall and drive her out of the room.

So the day passes, now in sorrow now in anger, and all the time I am waiting only for him to come home again. As the hour draws near, I begin to get ready. I have my bath, comb my hair, wear a new sari. I even apply a little scent. I begin to be very busy around the house, because I don't want it to be seen how much I am waiting for him. When I hear his footsteps, I am busier than ever and pretend not to hear them. He stands inside the door and raps his umbrella against it and calls out in a loud voice: "Is it safe to come in? Has the fury abated?" I try not to smile, but in spite of myself my mouth corners twitch.

After we have had a quarrel and have forgiven each other, we are always very gay together. These are our best times. We walk around the garden, my arm in his, he smoking a cigar and I chewing a betel leaf; he tells me some funny stories and makes me laugh so much that sometimes I have to stand still and hold my sides and gasp for air, while begging him to stop. Nobody ever sees us like this, in this mood; if they did, they would not wonder, as they all do, why we are living together. Yes, everyone asks this question, I know it very well, not only my people but his too – all his foreign friends who think he is miserable with me and that we do nothing but quarrel and that I am too stupid to be good company for him. Let them see us like this only once, then they would know; or afterward, when he allows me to come into his rooms and stay there with him the whole night.

It is quite different in his rooms from the rest of the house. The rest of the house doesn't have very much furniture in it, only some of our old things – some carved Kashmiri screens and little carved tables with mother-of-pearl tops. There are chairs and a few sofas, but I always feel most comfortable on the large mattress on the floor that is covered with an embroidered cloth and many bolsters and cushions; here I recline for hours, very comfortably, playing patience or cutting betel nuts with my little sil-

ver shears. But in his rooms there is a lot of furniture, and a ra-
diogram and a cabinet for his records and another for his bottles
of liquor. There are carpets and many pictures – some paintings
of European countryside and one old oil painting of a pink and
white lady with a fan and in old-fashioned dress. There is also a
framed pencil sketch of Boekelman himself, which was made by
a friend of his, a chemist from Vienna who was said to have been
a very good artist but died from heatstroke one very bad Delhi
summer. Hanging on the walls or standing on the mantelpiece or
on little tables all over the room are a number of photographs,
and these I like to look at even better than the paintings, because
they are all of him as a boy or as oh! such a handsome young man,
and of his parents and the hotel they owned and all lived in, in a
place called Zandvoort. There are other photographs in a big album, which he sometimes allows me to look at. In this album
there are also a few pictures of his wife ("Once bitten, twice
shy"), which I'm very interested in; but he never lets me look at
the album for long, because he is afraid I might spoil it, and he
takes it away from me and puts it back in the drawer where it belongs. He is neat and careful with all his things and gets very angry when they are disarranged by the servants during dusting;
yet he also insists on very thorough dusting, and woe to the
whole household if he finds some corner has been forgotten. So,
although there are so many things, it is always tidy in his rooms,
and it would be a pleasure to go in there if it were not for Susi.

He has always had a dog, and it has always been the same very
small, very hairy kind, and it has always been called Susi. This is
the second Susi I have known. The first died of very old age and
this Susi too is getting quite old now. Unfortunately dogs have a
nasty smell when they get old, and since Susi lives in Boekelman's rooms all the time, the rooms also have this smell although
they are so thoroughly cleaned every day. When you enter the
first thing you notice is this smell, and it always fills me with a
moment's disgust, because I don't like dogs and certainly would

never allow one inside a room. But for B. dogs are like his children. How he fondles his smelly Susi with her long hair, he bathes her with his own hands and brushes her and at night she sleeps on his bed. It is horrible. So when he lets me stay in his room in the night, Susi is always there with us, and she is the only thing that prevents me from being perfectly happy then. I think Susi also doesn't like it that I'm there. She looks at me from the end of the bed with her running eyes, and I can see that she doesn't like it. I feel like kicking her off the bed and out of the room and out of the house: but because that isn't possible I try and pretend she is not there. In any case, I don't have any time for her, because I am so busy looking at B. He is usually asleep before me, and then I sit up in bed beside him and look and look my eyes out at him. I can't describe how I feel. I have been a married woman, but I have never known such joy as I have in being there alone with him in bed and looking at him: at this old man who has taken his front teeth out so that his upper lip sags over his gums, his skin is grey and loose, he makes ugly sounds out of his mouth and nose as he sleeps. It is rapture for me to be there with him.

No one else ever sees him like this. All those friends he has, all his European lady friends – they only see him dressed up and with his front teeth in. And although they have known him all these years, longer than I have, they don't really know anything about him. Only the outer part is theirs, the shell, but what is within, the essence, that is known only to me. But they wouldn't understand that, for what do they know of outer part and inner, of the shell and of the essence! It is all one to them. For them it is only life in this world and a good time and food and drink, even though they are old women like me and should not have their thoughts on these things.

I have tried hard to like these friends of his, but it is not possible for me. They are very different from anyone else I know. They have all of them been in India for many, many years –

twenty-five, thirty – but I know they would much rather be somewhere else. They only stay here because they feel too old to go anywhere else and start a new life. They came here for different reasons – some because they were married to Indians, some to do business, others as refugees and because they couldn't get a visa for anywhere else. None of them has ever tried to learn any Hindi or to get to know anything about our India. They have some Indian "friends," but these are all very rich and important people – like maharanis and cabinet ministers, they don't trouble with ordinary people at all. But really they are only friends with one another, and they always like each other's company best. That doesn't mean they don't quarrel together, they do it all the time, and sometimes some of them are not on speaking terms for months or even years; and whenever two of them are together, they are sure to be saying something bad about a third. Perhaps they are really more like family than friends, the way they both love and hate each other and are closely tied together whether they like it or not; and none of them has any other family, so they are really dependent on each other. That's why they are always celebrating one another's birthday the way a family does, and they are always together on their big days like Christmas or New Year. If one of them is sick, the others are there at once with grapes and flowers, and sit all day and half the night around the sickbed, even if they have not been on speaking terms.

I know that Boekelman has been very close with some of the women, and there are a few of them who are still fond of him and would like to start all over again with him. But he has had enough of them – at least in that way, although of course he is still on very friendly terms with them and meets them every day almost. When he and I are alone together, he speaks of them very disrespectfully and makes fun of them and tells me things about them that no woman would like anyone to know. He makes me laugh, and I feel proud, triumphant, that he should be saying all this to me. But he never likes me to say anything about them, he gets very angry if I do and starts shouting that I have no right to talk, I don't know them and don't know all they have suffered; so I keep quiet, although often I feel very annoyed with them and would like to speak my mind.

The times I feel most annoyed is when there is a party in Boekelman's rooms and I'm invited there with them. They all have a good time, they eat and drink, tell jokes, sometimes they quarrel; they laugh a lot and kiss each other more than is necessary. No one takes much notice of me, but I don't mind that, I'm used to it with them; anyway, I'm busy most of the time running in and out of the kitchen to see to the preparations. I am glad I have something to do because otherwise I would be very bored only sitting there. What they say doesn't interest me, and their jokes don't make me laugh. Most of the time I don't understand what they are talking about, even when they are speaking in English – which is not always, for sometimes they speak in other languages such as French or German. But I always know, in whatever language they are speaking, when they start saying things about India. Sooner or later they always come to this subject, and then their faces change, they look mean and bitter like people who feel they have been cheated by some shopkeeper and it is too late to return the goods. Now it becomes very difficult for me to keep calm. How I hate to hear them talking in this way, saying that India is dirty and everyone is dishonest; but because they are my guests, they are in my house, I have to keep hold of myself and sit there with my arms folded. I must keep my eyes lowered, so that no one should see how they are blazing with fire. Once they have started on this subject, it always takes them a long time to stop, and the more they talk the more bitter they become, the expression on their faces becomes more and more unpleasant. I suffer, and yet I begin to see that they too are suffering, all the terrible things they are saying are not only against India but against themselves too – because they are here and have nowhere else to go – and against the fate that has brought them here and left them here, so far from where they belong and everything they hold dear.

Boekelman often talks about India in this way, but I have got used to it with him. I know very well that whenever something is not quite right – for instance, when a button is missing from his shirt, or it is a very hot day in summer – at once he will start saying how bad everything is in India. Well, with him I just laugh and take no notice. But once my eldest son, Shammi, overheard him and was so angry with him, as angry as I get with B.'s friends when I hear them talking in this way. It happened some years ago – it is painful for me to recall this occasion . . . .

Shammi was staying with me for a few days. He was alone that time, though often he used to come with his whole family, his wife, Monica, and my three darling grandchildren. Shammi is in the army – he was still a major then, though now he is a lieutenant colonel – which is a career he has wanted since he was a small boy and which he loves passionately. At the cadet school he was chosen as the best cadet of the year, for there was no one whose buttons shone so bright or who saluted so smartly as my Shammi. He is a very serious boy. He loves talking to me about his regiment and about tank warfare and 11-1 bore rifles and other such things, and I love listening to him. I don't really understand what he is saying, but I love his eager voice and the way he looks when he talks – just as he looked when he was a small boy and told me about his cricket. Anyway, this is what we were doing that morning, Shammi and I, sitting on the veranda, he talking and I looking sometimes at him and sometimes out into the garden, where everything was green and cool and birds bathed themselves in a pool of water that had oozed out of the hose pipe and sunk deep into the lawn.

This peace was broken by Boekelman. It started off with his shouting at the servant, very loudly and rudely, as he always does; nobody minds this, I don't mind it, the servant doesn't mind it, we are so used to it and we know it never lasts very long;

in any case, the servant doesn't understand what is said for it is always in English, or even some other language that none of us understands, and afterward, if he has shouted very loudly, Boekelman always gives the servant a little tip or one of his old shirts or pair of old shoes. But Shammi was very surprised for he had never heard him shout and abuse in this way (B. was always very careful how he behaved when any of the children were there). Shammi tried to continue talking to me about his regiment, but B. was shouting so loud that it was difficult to pretend not to hear him.

But it might still have been all right and nothing would have been said and Shammi and I could have pretended to each other that nothing had been heard if Boekelman had not suddenly come rushing out on to the veranda. He held his shaving brush in one hand, and half his face was covered in shaving lather and on the other half there was a spot of blood where he had cut himself; he was in his undervest and trousers, and the trousers had braces dangling behind like two tails. He had completely lost control of himself, I could see at once, and he didn't care what he said or before whom. He was so excited that he could hardly talk and he shook his shaving brush in the direction of the servant, who had followed him and stood helplessly watching him from the doorway. "These people!" he screamed. "Monkeys! Animals!" I didn't know what had happened but could guess that it was something quite trivial, such as the servant removing a razor blade before it was worn out. "Hundreds, thousands of times I tell them!" B. screamed, shaking his brush. "The whole country is like that! Idiots! Fools! Not fit to govern themselves!"

Shammi jumped up. His fists were clenched, his eyes blazed. Quickly I put my hand on his arm; I could feel him holding himself back, his whole body shaking with the effort. Boekelman did not notice anything but went on shouting, "Damn rotten backward country!" I kept my hand on Shammi's arm, though I could see he had himself under control now and was standing very straight and at attention, as if on parade, with his eyes fixed above Boekelman's head. "Go in now," I told B., trying to sound as if nothing very bad was happening, "at least finish your shaving." Boekleman opened his mouth to shout some more abuses, this time probably at me, but then he caught sight of Shammi's face and he remained with his mouth open. "Go in," I said to him again, but it was Shammi who went in and left us, turning suddenly on his heel and marching away with his strong footsteps. The screen door banged hard behind him on its spring hinges. Boekelman stood and looked after him, his mouth still open and the soap caking on his cheek. I went up close to him and shook my fist under his nose. "Fool!" I said to him in Hindi and with such violence that he took a step backward in fear. I didn't glance at him again but turned away and swiftly followed Shammi into the house.

Shammi was packing his bag. He wouldn't talk to me and kept his head averted from me while he took neat piles of clothes out of the drawer and packed them neatly into his bag. He has always been a very orderly boy. I sat on his bed and watched him. If he had said something, if he had been angry, it would have been easier; but he was quite silent, and I knew that under his shirt his heart was beating fast. When he was small and something had happened to him, he would never cry, but when I held him close to me and put my hand under his shirt I used to feel his heart beating wildly inside his child's body, like a bird in a frail cage. And now too I longed to do this, to lay my hand on his chest and soothe his suffering. Only now he was grown up, a big major with a wife and children, who had no need of his foolish mother anymore. And worse, much worse, now it was not something from outside that was the cause of his suffering, but I, I myself! When I thought of that, I could not restrain myself – a sob broke from me and I cried out "Son!" and next moment, before I knew myself what I was doing, I was down on the ground, holding his feet and bathing them with my tears to beg his forgiveness.

He tried to raise me, but I am a strong, heavy woman and I clung obstinately to his feet; so he too got down on the floor and in his effort to raise me took me in his arms. Then I broke into a storm of tears and hid my face against his chest, overcome with shame and remorse and yet also with happiness that he was so near to me and holding me so tenderly. We stayed like this for some time. At last I raised my head, and I saw tears on his lashes, like silver drops of dew. And these tender drops on his long lashes like a girl's, which always seem so strange in his soldier's face – these drops were such a burning reproach to me that at this moment I decided I must do what he wanted desperately, he and all my other children, and what I knew he had been silently asking of me since the day he came. I took the end of my sari and with it wiped the tears from his eyes and as I did this I said, "It's all right, son. I will tell him to go." And to reassure him, because he was silent and perhaps didn't believe me, I said, "Don't worry at all, I will tell him myself," in a firm, promising voice.

Shammi went home the next day. We did not mention the subject any more, but when he left he knew that I would not break my promise. And indeed that very day I went to Boekelman's room and told him that he must leave. It was a very quiet scene. I spoke calmly, looked not at B. but over his head, and he answered me calmly, saying very well, he would go. He asked only that I should give him time to find alternative accommodation, and of course to this I agreed readily, and we even had a quiet little discussion about what type of place he should look for. We spoke like two acquaintances, and everything seemed very nice till I noticed that, although his voice was quite firm and he was talking so reasonably, his hands were slightly trembling. Then my feelings changed, and I had quickly to leave the room in order not to give way to them.

From now on he got up earlier than usual in the mornings and went out to look for a place to rent. He would raise his hat to me as he passed me sitting on the veranda, and sometimes we would have a little talk together, mainly about the weather, before he passed on, raising his hat again and with Susi on the lead walking behind him, her tail in the air. The first few days he seemed very cheerful, but after about a week I could see he was tired of going out so early and never finding anything, and Susi too seemed tired and her tail was no longer so high. I hardened my heart against them. I could guess what was happening – how he went from place to place and found everywhere the rents were very high and the accommodation very small compared with the large rooms he had had in my house all these years for almost nothing. Let him learn, I thought to myself and said nothing except "Good morning" and "The weather is changing fast, soon it will be winter" as I watched him going with slower and slower footsteps day after day out of the gate.

At last one day he confessed to me that, in spite of all his efforts, he had not yet succeeded in finding anything suitable. He had some hard things to say about rapacious landlords. I listened patiently but did not offer to extend his stay. My silence prompted him to stand on his pride and say that I need not worry, that very shortly he would definitely be vacating the rooms. And indeed only two days later he informed me that although he had not yet found any suitable place, he did not want to inconvenience me any further and had therefore made an alternative arrangement, which would enable him to leave in a day or two. Of course I should have answered only "Very well" and inclined my head in a stately manner, but like a fool instead I asked, "What alternative arrangement?" This gave him the opportunity to be stately with me; he looked at me in silence for a moment and then gave a little bow and, raising his hat, proceeded toward the gate with Susi. I bit my lip in anger. I would have liked to run after him and shout as in the old days, but instead I had to sit there by myself and brood. All day I brooded what alternative arrangement he could have made. Perhaps he was going to a hotel, but I didn't think so, because hotels nowa-

days are very costly, and although he is not poor, the older he
gets the less he likes to spend.

In the evening his friend Lina came to see him. There was a lot
of noise from his rooms and also some thumping, as of suitcases
being taken down; Lina shouted and laughed at the top of her
voice, as she always does. I crept halfway down the stairs and
tried to hear what they were saying. I was very agitated. As soon
as she had gone, I walked into his room – without knocking,
which was against his strict orders – and at once demanded,
standing facing him with my hands at my waist, "You are not
moving in with *Lina*?" Some of his pictures had already been removed from the walls and his rugs rolled up; his suitcases stood
open and ready.

Although I was very heated, he remained calm. "Why not
Lina?" he asked, and looked at me in a mocking way.

I made a sound of contempt. Words failed me. To think of
him living with Lina, in her two furnished rooms that were already overcrowded with her own things and always untidy! And
Lina herself, also always untidy, her hair blond when she remembered to dye it, her swollen ankles, and her loud voice and
laugh! She had first come to India in the 1930s to marry an Indian, a boy from a very good family, but he left her quite
soon – of course, how could a boy like that put up with her ways?
She is very free with men, even now though she is old and ugly,
and I know she has liked B. for a long time. I was quite deter-
mined on one thing; never would I allow him to move to her
place, even if it meant keeping him here in the house with me for
some time longer.

But when I told him that where was the hurry, he could wait
till he found a good place of his own, then he said thank you, he
had made his arrangements, and as I could see with my own eyes
he had already begun to pack up his things; and after he had said
that, he turned away and began to open and shut various drawers
and take out clothes, just to show me how busy he was with pack-

ing. He had his back to me, and I stood looking at it and longed to thump it.

The next day too Lina came to the house and again I heard her talking and laughing very loudly, and there was some banging about as if they were moving the suitcases. She left very late at night, but even after she had gone I could not sleep and tossed this side and that on my bed. I no longer thought of Shammi but only of B. Hours passed, one o'clock, two o'clock, three, still I could not sleep. I walked up and down my bedroom, then I opened the door and walked up and down the landing. After a while it seemed to me I could hear sounds from downstairs, so I crept halfway down the stairs to listen. There was some movement in his room, and then he coughed also, a very weak cough, and he cleared his throat as if it were hurting him. I put my ear to the door of his room; I held my breath, but I could not hear anything further. Very slowly I opened the door. He was sitting in a chair with his head down and his arms hanging loose between his legs, like a sick person. The room was in disorder, with the rugs rolled up and the suitcases half packed, and there were glasses and an empty bottle, as if he and Lina had been having a party. There was also the stale smoke of her cigarettes; she never stops smoking and then throws the stubs, red with lipstick, anywhere she likes.

He looked up for a moment at the sound of the door opening, but when he saw it was I he looked down again without saying anything. I tiptoed over to his armchair and sat at his feet on the floor. My hand slowly and soothingly stroked his leg, and he allowed me to do this and did not stir. He stared in front of him with dull eyes; he had his teeth out and looked an old, old man. There was no need for us to say anything, to ask questions and give answers. I knew what he was thinking as he stared in front of him in this way, and I too thought of the same thing. I thought of him gone away from here and living with Lina, or alone with his dog in some rented room; no contact with India or Indians, no words to communicate with except *achchha* (all right) and *pani* (water); no one to care for him as he grew older and older, and perhaps sick, and his only companions people just like himself—as old, as lonely, as disappointed, and as far from home.

He sighed, and I said, "Is your indigestion troubling you?" although I knew it was something worse than only indigestion. But he said yes, and added, "It was the spinach you made them cook for my supper. How often do I have to tell you I can't digest spinach at night." After a while he allowed me to help him into bed. When I had covered him and settled his pillows the way he liked them, I threw myself on the bed and begged, "Please don't leave me."

"I've made my arrangements," he said in a firm voice. Susi, at the end of the bed, looked at me with her running eyes and wagged her tail as if she were asking for something.

"Stay," I pleaded with him. "Please stay."

There was a pause. At last he said, as if he were doing me a big favor, "Well, we'll see"; and added, "Get off my bed now, you're crushing my legs—don't you know what a big heavy lump you are?"

None of my children ever comes to stay with me now. I know they are sad and disappointed with me. They want me to be what an old widowed mother should be, devoted entirely to prayer and self-sacrifice; I too know it is the only state fitting to this last stage of life that I have now reached. But that great all-devouring love that I should have for God, I have for B. Sometimes I think: perhaps this is the path for weak women like me? Perhaps B. is a substitute for God whom I should be loving, the way the little brass image of Vishnu in my prayer room is a substitute for that great god himself? These are stupid thoughts that sometimes come to me when I am lying next to B. on his bed and looking at him and feeling so full of peace and joy that I wonder how I came to be so, when I am living against all right rules and the wishes of my children. How do I deserve the great happiness that I find in that old man? It is a riddle.

The Neighbors

* * * * *

Yasunari Kawabata was one of Japan's most distinguished novelists and winner of the 1968 Nobel
Prize for Literature. He was born in 1899, and died,
by his own hand, in 1972. Among his better known
works are *Snow Country*, *Thousand
Cranes*, and *The Master of Go*.

*I*F IT'S YOU, the old folks will be happy, too," said Murano, looking at the newlyweds Kichirō and Yukiko. "Both my father and mother are almost completely deaf. It sounds funny to
say this, but please don't worry about anything."

For work reasons, Murano had moved to Tokyo. His old father and mother remained at the house in Kamakura. They lived
in the detached wing. That was why he was choosing tenants for
the main house. Rather than close the house up, it was better to
have people living in it. For the old people, too, it was less lonely. The rent was nominal. The go-between in the marriage talks
of the young couple, an acquaintance of Murano's, had acted as
an intermediary here, also. When Kichirō, with Yukiko, had
gone to see Murano, they had been favorably received.

"It'll be like a flower suddenly blooming alongside the old
folks. I hadn't been looking especially for newlyweds, but, if I
can have you living there, both the old house and the old folks

will be bathed in the sunshine of your youth. I can almost see it," Murano said.

The house of Kamakura was at the head of one of the many valleys thereabouts. The main house, with its six rooms, was too large for the young couple. The night of their arrival, unused to the house and the quiet, they turned on all the lights in the six rooms. With lights on even in the kitchen and the earthen entry-way, they sat in the twelve-mat parlor. Although it was the larg-est room in the house, what with Yukiko's armoire, dressing stand, bedding, and the other articles of her dowry that had been brought in here for the time being, there was hardly any room to sit. It made the two feel at home.

Arranging the loose "dragonfly jewels" of her broken necklace in various combinations, Yukiko was trying to piece together a new necklace. Of the two or three hundred of these old glass beads that her father had collected among the natives during his four or five years in Taiwan, Yukiko had been given sixteen or seventeen of her favorites before her marriage. Stringing them together in a necklace, she'd taken them with her on her honey-moon. As her father's prized curios, those dragonfly jewels sym-bolized for Yukiko the emotion of parting from her parents. The morning after the bridal night, Yukiko had put the necklace on. Attracted by it, Kichirō had embraced Yukiko, pressing his face against her neck. Yukiko, tickled, had pulled away from him with a little scream. The thread of the necklace had snapped. The beads had scattered all over the floor.

"Ahhh!" Kichirō let go of Yukiko. Squatting, the two had gathered up the fallen beads. Yukiko, unable to hold back her laughter at Kichirō crawling around on his hands and knees in search of the beads, suddenly relaxed.

The beads differed in color, pattern, and shape. There were round ones, square ones, and slender tube-shaped ones. The colors – red, blue, purple, yellow, and such – were simple primary colors, and yet, with time, they'd all taken on a subdued, mellow hue. The patterns of the beads, too, had the naive charm of native art. As one subtly varied the arrangement of the beads, the feeling of the necklace also changed subtly. Designed by the natives to be strung on necklaces, each bead had a hole in it for the thread to pass through.

As Yukiko tried changing the arrangement this way and that, Kichirō asked, "Don't you remember the original arrangement?"

"My father and I did it together, so I don't remember everything. I'll string them together in a new way that you like. Please have a look at them."

Shoulder pressed to shoulder, they forgot the passage of time in the arrangement of the dragonfly jewels. The night grew late.

"Isn't something walking around outside?" Yukiko listened. There was the scurrying sound of dead leaves. Leaves seemed to be falling, not on the roof of this house, but on the roof of the detached wing in back. The wind had risen.

The next morning, Yukiko called out to Kichirō.

"Come here, come here quickly! The old folks in back are feeding a couple of black kites. The kites are having breakfast with them."

When Kichirō got up and went outside, he saw that the doors of the detached wing were all open in the mild, clear autumn daylight. In the sun that shone into the breakfast room, the old husband and wife were having their breakfast. The detached wing stood on a slight rise from the garden, set off from it by a low hedge of mountain tea flower. Since the hedge was in full bloom, the detached wing seemed to float above a bank of flowers. On three sides it was surrounded, as if about to be buried, by the mixed forest of the low mountain in its fall colors. The late-autumn morning sunlight, shining through the tea flower hedge and the fall foliage, seemed to warm them to their innermost depths.

The two kites, approaching the breakfast table, lifted their heads. The old couple, chewing up the ham and omelet on their plates, held it out to them between their chopsticks. Each time they did so, the birds would spread their wings a little.

"They're so tame," Kichirō said. "Let's go over and say hello. It's during breakfast, but I don't think they'll mind. I'd like to meet their beloved birds."

Going inside, Yukiko changed into day clothes. When she came out, she was wearing the necklace they'd worked on so hard the night before.

At the sound of their approach to the tea flower hedge, the two birds suddenly took flight. Their beating wings startled the young couple's ears. Exclaiming "Ahhh," Yukiko looked up as the kites ascended into the sky. Evidently they were mountain kites who had come down to the old folks' place.

Painstakingly expressing their gratitude at being allowed to live in the main house, Kichirō said, "I'm sorry I scared the birds away. They've certainly taken to you."

But the old people didn't seem to have heard anything. Apparently not even trying to hear, they gazed emptily at the young couple. Turning to Kichirō, Yukiko asked him with her eyes what to do.

"It was very good of you to come. Mother – this beautiful young couple are our neighbors now." The old man spoke abruptly, as if to himself. But his wife didn't seem to hear this either.

"Old deaf folks like us – you can think of us as not being here. But we like to see young people. We won't make any trouble for you, but we won't hide ourselves away."

Kichirō and Yukiko bowed their heads.

A kite was circling high over the roof of the cottage. It cried out with a sweet voice.

"The kites haven't finished their breakfast. They've come down from the mountain again. We musn't be in their way." Kichirō, urging Yukiko, got to his feet.

Translated by L ANE D UNLOP

An Unfinished Record

✳   ✳   ✳   ✳   ✳

Zhang Jie did not publish her first story until she
was over 40 and after China's Cultural Revolution.
Since then she has been surrounded by controversy
and does not hesitate to take on social themes in her
work. *Love Must Not Be Forgotten*, her first work to
be published in the U.S., includes a novella
and six stories.

I KNOW that I will never come back to this place again. As I
close the window, forcing my old cat, The Grand Historian, outside for the last time, he grows cross with me for the insult of
this rough treatment. Yet he's far too tolerant and dignified to
scratch or yowl at me. He merely springs back onto the windowsill, crouched, staring at me through the pane, with those apparently all-seeing eyes.

The sighing of the poplars, the clamor of the traffic, the neighbor boy playing his mouth-organ are all muffled now, more distant, removed. I wonder if the lad is growing tired, attempting
the same tune over and over again since this morning. But I am
finished with these sounds by now and with the pain they make
deep inside my ears.

I decide to be thorough and lock the window, but it's been
broken for so long that the frame is coming apart and is too mis-
shapen to shut properly. No matter how hard I try, it cannot be
bolted. It is not the fault of the maintenance staff for not doing

their job properly, rather I'd call it one more symptom of my hopeless indifference to making my life more comfortable. Usually I managed by tying up the frame with string, making raising the window a terrible nuisance, but luckily I've rarely opened it. I've long been as delicate as a premature baby and the night breezes or the slightest change in temperature cause me the most mysterious complaints. I'm always wishing our hospitals had insulated cubicles for decrepit old wrecks like me to find rest in.

From being shut off so long my room has always had a musty atmosphere, like that of a cellar, the desiccated odor of a room where an invalid has been enduring for a long time. But for the last few nights I've kept the window open, wanting the flower-scented spring breeze to drift into every corner and whisk away all traces of my life which has impregnated the room for all these years. It was a warm, lovely breeze but it started me off coughing, my throat thick with phlegm, like a chimney clogged with soot. If only, like a chimney, it could be swept clean.

This is probably the last thing I will be able to do for anyone else. Or is it the first? The best thing, of course, would have been to give these walls a good new coat of whitewash, but now it's too late. Sooner or later some new tenants will move in, and I don't wish them to resent any lingering part of me. But even if they do resent any hold I may have on the place, I will be beyond hearing them.

The hospital called me the day before yesterday with the message that I should come there today. The boy who spoke to me had a voice like a singer in a musical, melodious, as though he were singing a solo. He might have been urging me to go to a rendezvous with someone who'd be waiting for me, under a silk tree or by a little bridge. But instead I'll be going through the door that leads to. . . who can say what.

After that phone call I began looking back over my life, the way people who are about to die find themselves doing. It surprised me – why hadn't I done this before? Do we really have to wait until it's too late to do anything, before we remember all those countless old debts great and small that we've no way of settling now? Each of us can only experience the mystery of death once and it seems cruel to enter this mystery feeling unsettled, with a sense of guilt. But, in fact, my life has been pointless and dull, the most ordinary life possible, containing absolutely nothing of interest for a novelist – no dramatic tragedy, no peaks of joy. Poor soul who must write my eulogy, perhaps the shortest eulogy ever, read in two brief minutes.

My very name seems to have been designed to make things awkward for everyone. It's graceless, hard to pronounce, a stiff and commonplace-sounding name. Even though it appears on the spine of books on Ming history every couple of years or so, those thick tomes of four or five hundred pages costing well over a yuan are usually found on the bottom shelves of the bookshop. I always know perfectly well that when my next book comes out the previous one won't have sold out, but I can't help going to the bookshop from time to time to look and see if there are any fewer of those unsold volumes. Even one less would be a welcome sight. Then I slip away like a thief, afraid someone will discover that I'm the author of those unsold books. I've wasted all that paper, I feel, and tricked my readers into giving me their time. It makes me heavy-hearted. I know I have little talent, but it's as if I had been bewitched into devoting all my thoughts, my soul and even my body to the study of our ancestors' history. I could not stop myself from writing. What else was there for me to live for, all alone as I am?

A moment ago Li, my neighbor, asked with some concern whether there was anything he could do for me while I was in hospital. Should he take letters and cables straight to the hospital, or wait till he could bring them along when he came to visit me? They could wait, I told him. He could get someone to take them along when it was convenient.

Apart from letters to and from publishers, magazines and a

university journal which takes my articles, and very occasionally
a handwritten note from another simple-minded bookworm like
me wanting to argue about just where a battle was fought during
some dynasty, I have virtually no private correspondence. And
since I have done no work for a long time because of my illness,
even letters such as these have become few and far between.

Now that I think of it, there is something to be said for having
no private life: You have few attachments, and nobody has to
feel distressed when you begin to fail. Still, if I do get to heaven I
shall feel sad that no one on earth will be grieving for me. It's not
that I don't get along with people, but that I simply haven't had
the good fortune to make any friends. My colleagues in the research institute regard me with great respect and kindness.
People usually treat me well, but I tend to frighten them off, or
to mistake their ordinary courtesy for an expression of interest.
I'm afraid I have gone on for hours and hours citing evidence to
show that the Qing historian Xia Xie's *Universal Mirror of Ming
History* is full of wrong judgments, not caring whether my listen-
ers are interested, how busy they are, or if I'm trying their patience. Whenever I have to return a visit, my mind stays back
with those manuscripts piled on my desk and I hope that the person I am going to see will be out. Then, by leaving a brief note I
can meet the requirements of courtesy with the minimum waste
of time. If I find them in I always make meaningless remarks,
such as "It's gradually been getting a bit warmer recently," then
repeat myself three times over. These social performances generally exhaust me, and my boorishness and lack of manners leave
others at a complete loss as to how to deal with me. When I get up
to leave, my host's face shows relief and gratitude that he will not
have to prolong this mutual torture.

My everday life is totally organized around work, and on public holidays when I can't go to the institute cafeteria, I'm never
sure about when to eat breakfast, lunch, or supper. No one has
more enthusiasm than I have for the development of China's

food and clothing industries: I'm eager for the time when the whole business of eating can be reduced to the simplicity of the astronaut's toothpaste-tube meals. I await anxiously the new clothing to be made out of paper, as well as the quilt covers and pillowcases, so mine won't always be like soiled rags. Of course, I like clean clothes and quilt covers the same as everyone else, but I've had neither the time nor the inclination to bother with them.

But now these minor irritations are history and I ask myself: Has there been nothing else interesting to review from my life? Is there no more than the few yuan I owe here and there, or the call I've forgotten to return? In a fairy tale of Hans Christian Andersen, one cold, winter's night a lonely old man on the point of death sees the whole of the past through one of his cloudy tears. And it reminds me that there has been just one tear in my long, monotonous life. Not an old man's cloudy tear, but a unique tear from my youth that had the luster and the color of a pearl. It is only now, when it is about to be buried with me, that I can bear to bring it up from the deep well of memory.

It was a warm summer morning. She was laughing as she came into our office which was dark and sombre from the shadowy green vines on the wall outside the small windows. From the moment she arrived it was as if there had been another window in the room. How could she laugh so much? Whenever she laughed I laughed too, and I discovered to my delight that this made her laugh even more. I never knew what I looked like when I laughed, but from then on I was full of confidence that my face looked fine when I laughed, and that confidence made my writing suddenly speed up from one to two thousand characters a day.

I'm always losing umbrellas, one after another. It only has to rain for me to lose an umbrella – on buses, in little restaurants or bookstores I chance upon, or by newsstands. The day I left my umbrella at some academic conference, she came running after me, calling and laughing, and handed me my umbrella back. I drank in her laughter with such pleasure that I forgot to thank her.

LISTENING TO HER VOICE, to her laughter, and feeling that the office had an extra window in it had become the most important thing in my life. Any day on which she did not come to work might just as well have not happened. Her lightness, her conversation, her losing a button, her touch of irritation because she had been unable to buy a pretty pair of shoes all slowly infused the historical data I read and the words I wrote. I longed to share everything I had and everything I did with her.

My life seemed a lot more complicated than it had been before I knew her. I was always showing her books that I found interesting and useful, and whenever I talked to her about our admirable forebears and the history that had ebbed like a tide I felt an emotion I had never known before: happiness.

I even started going to the pictures. I recall one film. At the time everyone said that it was a thoroughly boring film, the sort you forget all about before you're even outside the cinema. But that film, with an actress who reminded me of her, turned my heart upside down. I found a new boldness I didn't know I had. I took out paper and pen and I wrote to her, asking her to meet at nine o'clock by a little bridge, just as in the film. Even the words I used were borrowed from the film. I was drunk with the image of her running to meet me under the silk tree.

I arrived an hour early, to be there ready, to see her as she arrived. Nine o'clock passed. By ten o'clock she had still not come and I thought that I must have written the wrong date or time. That was very possible, even though I had taken the letter out of the envelope many times, read it through and put it back again before I posted it. I could not be sure that my mind had been clear enough at the time, or whether my nerves had been dependable. That sort of thing had happened to me before. Back in middle-school math, for example, an exam question asked what 50/2 was equal to. I wrote it correctly: 50/2. I don't know how many times I checked through my answers, but for its own reasons my mind stubbornly held onto 50/3, a fraction that could not be reduced any further. Could I in the same way have written midday or 8 p.m. instead of 9 a.m.?

I became hungry, but I dared not leave the little bridge to have some lunch. I kept taking my glasses off to wipe clean the lenses, so I wouldn't miss seeing her, but they stayed as hazy as ever. I wished I had not always thrust them into my pockets with keys, nailclippers and everything else, or carelessly thrown them lensdown on my desk, until they were like frosted glass. Why did they seem now even worse than ever?

I began to wonder whether she had suddenly fallen ill. I felt so anxious that my heart was hurting. Perhaps she had an accident on the way there. If something like that really had happened I'd never have been able to forgive myself, not even if I could have gone to hell and been punished ten times over.

The bustle of traffic and people gradually died away with the day. The street lights came on in the distance and generously cast their gentle orange glow over me, as if to soothe away my disappointment. I walked home alone, among the shadows, as if the happiness of the morning had never been.

Even before I got into the office next morning I heard her laughter as I walked on the path among the green trees. Thank heavens! She was still alive, healthy and happy. For a long time I stood under the eaves of the building, not wanting to go inside in case some other impression might weaken the happiness I had lost and now recovered. My eyes were filled with tears of gratitude, even though I did not know who I should be thanking or for what.

Laughing as sweetly as ever she spoke to me, "Please meet my fiancé. We would like you to come to our wedding on Saturday evening." He was strong, tall and good-looking and shook my hand heartily.

As she spoke she handed me a heavy parcel, wrapped in strong brown paper and tied with string. It was the book I had lent her. As I watched them I thought happily about their wedding, and of how well-matched they were. It was just as if my agonies of self-reproach by the bridge the day before had never happened and the letter I had tortured myself for so long over sending had never existed.

The wedding ceremony was informal, with a very free and jovial atmosphere, like a group of friends meeting spontaneously. That was very much her way of doing things. It was the first time I had been in a crowd without feeling awkward and uncomfortable.

The bridegroom sat down right next to me and told me he was a geologist. He explained to me with great gusto how the stress that caused earthquakes is built up, and how infrared remote sensing was going to replace the geologist's compass, hammer, and magnifying-glass in prospecting for the earth's natural resources. He talked to me not as if he were the groom, but as if he were a guest who had come along to offer his congratulations.

I smiled. His way of making conversation without bothering whether he was killing the person he was talking to was a bit like mine. He was very fond of his work and believed that geology was definitely very useful to the world and a truly wonderful science. I admired him and even started wondering whether I had made a mistake in studying history instead of geology all those years ago. He casually handed me a cigarette. He was evidently too happy and enthusiastic to care about such details as whether I was a smoker or wanted to smoke.

Of course I accepted the cigarette – I couldn't turn his kind offer down. He was the man she loved, and on top of that I liked him myself. I didn't know whether I was meant to swallow the evil-smelling fumes or to inhale them. From the health posters I had seen in hospitals about smoking causing lung cancer I guessed that you had to draw them into your lungs. I could not have remembered wrongly; the hospital was a place I knew very well, the place I went to most often apart from my office and my room. I choked on the first puff, but tried as hard as I could not to cough although the effort made my eyes water. It did not go at all well and I was afraid all this would alarm him and make him blame himself for causing one such misery.

She came over to us smiling, her eyes dazzling. She handed me an exquisite crystal glass and wanted me to drink a toast to them. I accepted the glass of wine and at once a humming started in my head. The drink was so strong, yet my heart remained light. It was very odd that I should have felt that way, but I was as happy as if I were getting married myself.

It was late at night when I left the place where those two people had surrounded me with happiness. It was mid-October, still quite warm, and I was in a cheerful frame of mind. I flung my jacket over my shoulders and strolled back through the moonlight. I didn't know whether it came from the cigarette or the drink, but I felt as if I were floating through the air. In a gust of light breeze I seemed to hear people whispering or laughing quietly from the locust and poplar trees by the roadside.

I remembered the Schubert Serenade stanzas the bridegroom had just been singing:

> *Softly my songs*
> *Cry to you through the night*

And I remembered her expression as he sang.

A pale longing welled up in my heart. I longed to have a soft shoulder beside me, longed to have someone leaning her adorable curly head against my shoulder. I would have put my jacket around her like a gallant Spanish knight wrapping his woman in his cloak.

I tripped over a stone, and looked down to see my shadow on

the ground, the shoulders as narrow as a child's. I looked as if I had three less ribs than anyone else, and seemed to be painfully bent forward. It suddenly occurred to me that I was an old fool – no woman would ever want to rest her head on a shoulder like mine.

> *Oh my dearest, a cry to the beloved is carried on the*
> *wind, on such a night as this....*

As soon as I was back in my room I flung myself across my little bed, stretched out to the side of the bedside table, and on it wrote the first letter of her name: S. I felt no particular misery or grief. Gradually my eyes misted up, and the letter seemed to turn into a winged angel flying lightly above my head. I closed my tired eyelids. I must have had a happy dream that night, but it was such a long time ago that I can no longer remember it clearly.

She soon left our institute and started travelling all over the country with her geologist. And the years passed. I realize that by now she must be as decrepit as I am, but as long as I don't see her again I'll remember her as she was when we parted, always laughing for no good reason, radiant and cheerful like someone who has slept and dreamt well the night before.

People say that love is endless longing, heartache and madness, wild exhilaration, pain like hell frozen over, cruel sleepless nights. I've never in all my life experienced such complicated and bittersweet emotions. But I am very grateful to her. Even though I never stood in front of her window night after night waiting for her shadow to appear, she still brought me good fortune. Because of her I knew the delight and felt the brightness that emanate from an extra window, and was happy even with just her single initial by my side.

I SUPPOSE I should be going, but there is still so much unfinished business to be done. Why am I trying to sort it out now in this last minute? I had intended to catalogue all the books now shoved into the shelves at random, and to arrange them by period so that they will be easier for their next owner to refer to. And I haven't yet corrected the proofs of the article on Zhu Yuanzhang, the founder of the Ming dynasty, and the Red Turban Army of peasants rebels.

All I managed to complete last night were two small tasks that were within my powers. I rubbed out the initial written on the side of my table, and burned that sheet of brown wrapping paper – so brittle it went to pieces at the touch – and the piece of string. I didn't want those things I've treasured for so many years to be casually thrown away as rubbish when my effects are sorted out after I'm dead, and I wasn't prepared to let a stranger's hand rub that initial out.

As I watched the last spark fly away I thought of all those years, of how I kept them as treasures because she had breathed on them and touched them. It was as if I had been a thief all these years, a thief who had stolen what she had never given me, what had never belonged to me – a tiny fragment of her life. It was probably the most shameful thing I have ever done. If I could I'd kneel before her and beg her to forgive me. She is so good and sweet and generous that I'm sure she'd have forgiven me and said, "In a long life everyone does something wrong."

As I lift the net bag with my washing things in it my toothbrush slips out through a hole and when I lean over to pick it up I take another look around the room that has shared half a lifetime with me. My old table stands isolated in the middle of the room, there irrelevant and unconnected, like some obscure island in the Pacific that not even the most third-rate explorer would bother with. The springs of my folding bed gave out a long time ago, and it sags very low to the floor. The yellowing and blackened walls have an air of decrepitude, just like my dried-up face, as they lean feebly together around my jumble of furniture. Even the books on the shelves look sick and crippled, without even one fine leather volume with gold lettering to give the bookshelves a touch of distinction. All the large softcover books lie on their sides, drooping out over the shelves like wilting foliage taken too long ago from a tree. Dusty cobwebs sway from the ceiling and in the corners of the room.

The sight of this dispirited room fills me with regret, as if I have wasted its youth for nothing. It could have been as clean, bright, and tidy as other rooms. And as I see this, a new nameless feeling begins to overwhelm me. I cannot give it a name, but from it I sense that my whole life from beginning to end has been lacking in something.

Lacking what? My eyes sweep the cluttered bookcases, across the books I've scrimped and saved for a lifetime to buy, or written with my own sweat and blood. I realize that I have all of these things to leave to a lot of people, but no one unique thing to leave to one special person. And this is the lack, this is what is missing.

I know that Dong from the personnel department of the institute will finally sign in the space on the operation form where the next of kin's signature is needed. But if only there could be one beloved face, wrinkled like mine, sitting on the bench outside the operating theater, anxious for me, quietly sobbing for me. If only on my bedside table there could be good things to eat prepared by her own hand. My head, which has worked through mountains of wastepaper like a mechanical recording machine, has at last shown its boundless creative genius in imagining the food. These delectable treats look, smell, and taste delicious as I eat them from the aluminum canteen that's been scrubbed till it shines.

But, in fact, the time for these imaginings is finished. Soon my ashes will lie in their urn which will be placed on an obscure shelf to gather dust for three years, until at last they are flung away.

Nobody will want to keep them. And even less will anyone want to mingle her ashes with mine.

There is a soft noise at the window. The Grand Historian's ugly face is pressed against the glass, his expression one of concentration and bewilderment. His usual coldness and superiority have vanished. I look away at once, not wanting him to see the loneliness in my heart. We have seen many things together and he should not feel bereft as I leave him. He scratches at the pane with his front paws like someone knocking at a door.

Years ago I picked him up in the street and brought him home. There wasn't an uglier, lazier cat in the world. His short tail was like a piece of rag. His greyish, dull fur was so dirty that you couldn't tell his true color. He had been sitting in the middle of the road, not moving or making a sound, while the torrent of bicycle, lorry, and car wheels flowed past him. He just sat there like a pile of rubbish that had been dumped on the road, as if he had stopped caring whether he lived or died. It would only have taken a small turn by a single wheel to squash him flat.

I gave him a bath in my foot-bowl and I'm inclined to think he failed to understand my good intentions and reckoned that I was trying to skin him alive. He drew blood where he clawed the back of my hand as he jumped onto my radio, which was playing at the time and felt warm to his paws. He stared at me with caution and silence. After several days of very close observation he acknowledged me as a friend, but even then, with a touch of condescension. Whenever I sat at my desk writing furiously he always looked at me with a certain superciliousness. His manner said: "What you're scribbling is all useless nonsense, old friend." When I read my articles aloud to myself, wagging my head, he lazily shut his eyes and purred rhythmically. And when I gazed with adoration at the letter written on the side of the table every night before going to sleep he sat by my pillow with his head on his front paws and stared at my face with a pitying, mocking stare. I am still covered from head to foot with little red flea bites, just as I was when he first came to me.

Every morning he used to stroke my thinning white hair with his paw, telling me to stop lying in bed gazing vacantly at the ceiling. Whenever I sat down to take a rest and shut my dim old eyes he'd spring onto my lap, or lick my hands with their protruding blue veins and slack, wrinkled skin, or grasp my wrists and nip my fingers, but very carefully so that he never hurt me.

It was because of him that I finally started paying some attention to feeding us properly and sometimes treated us with cold meat. I would spread it out on the greasy wrapping paper, and as he crouched on the other side of it facing me, we would take our time savoring the meat together. Sometimes my imagination would run free and I'd think that if we could both have had a drink we would have clinked glasses and drunk to each other. Thank God for sending me an animal soul, so patient and understanding, never using its tongue to harass or harm me. I am praying that the next tenant will adopt The Grand Historian and that maybe even he will liven up a bit. I'm sure he can, and that someone will take him in, but I can't be certain.

I have been silently hoping that the next tenant will be someone full of life who will decorate this room like other rooms with sheer white curtains, a gleaming crystal fixture hanging from the ceiling, a woven tablecloth, a beautiful landscape painting on the wall, and a vase of pale yellow roses . . . . A girl would be best. She'd be bound to have her boyfriend mend the window bolt so she could open it wide and allow the moonlight to come flooding in, the breeze to waft in the scent of locust blossom in May, and perhaps even strains of Schubert's Serenade. Then the room will have the joy and pleasure I was never able to bring to it.

What else is there left? Oh, yes, so many longings I still feel, vividly, acutely, now that the time is used up. They have not faded but hang suspended in my heart.

I used to think that all my emotions belonged in the past, to history, but I know that I yearn for the future just like everyone else. Even as life draws to a close, I realize that I have never understood myself completely .... If only ...

But now it certainly is too late to do more, to be more to this lifetime.

Translated by W.J.F. JENNER

IV

Clocks Like Horses

✳   ✳   ✳   ✳   ✳

Mohammed Khudayyir was born in southern Iraq
near Bastra where he now works as a schoolteacher.
He has published two volumes of short stories, *The
Black Kingdom* and *At a Temperature of
45° Centigrade*.

*T*HIS MEETING may take place. I shall get my watch re-
paired and go out to the quays of the harbour, then at the end of
the night I shall return to the hotel and find him sleeping in my
bed, his face turned to the wall, having hung his red turban on
the clothes hook.

Till today I still own a collection of old watches; I had come by
them from an uncle of mine who used to be a sailor on the ships
of the Andrew Weir company; old pocket watches with chains
and silver-plated cases, all contained in a small wooden box in
purses of shiny blue cloth. While my interest in them has of late
waned, I had, as a schoolboy, been fascinated by them. I would
take them out from their blue purses and scrutinize their work-
ings in an attempt to discover something about them that would
transcend "time stuffed like old cotton in a small cushion," as I
had recorded one day in my diary.

One day during the spring school holidays I was minded to remove one of these watches from its box and to put it into the
pocket of my black suit, attaching its chain to the buttonholes of

my waistcoat. For a long time I wandered round the chicken market before seating myself at a café. The waiter came and asked me the time. I calmly took the watch out of its blue purse. My watch was incapable of telling the time, like the other watches in the box, nothing in it working except for the spring of the case which was no sooner pressed than it flicked open revealing a pure white dial and two hands that stood pointing to two of the Roman numerals on the face. Before I could inform him that the watch was not working, the waiter had bent down and pulled the short chain towards him; having looked attentively at the watch he closed its case on which had been engraved a sailing ship within a frame of foreign writing. Then, giving it back to me, he stood up straight.

"How did you get hold of it?"

"I inherited it from a relative of mine."

I returned the watch to its place.

"Was your relative a sailor?"

"Yes."

"Only three or four of the famous sailors are still alive."

"My relative was called Mughamis."

"Mughamis? I don't know him."

"He wouldn't settle in one place. He died in Bahrain."

"That's sailors for you! Do you remember another sailor called Marzouk? Since putting ashore for the last time he has been living in Fao. He opened a shop there for repairing watches, having learned the craft from the Portuguese. He alone would be able to repair an old watch like yours."

I drank down the glass of tea and said to the waiter as I paid him: "Did you say he was living in Fao?"

"Yes, near the hotel."

The road to Fao is a muddy one and I went on putting off the journey until one sunny morning I took my place among the passengers in a bus which set off loaded with luggage. The passengers, who sat opposite one another in the middle of the bus, exchanged no words except for general remarks about journeying in winter, about how warm this winter was, and other comments about the holes in the road. At the moment they stopped talking I took out my watch. Their eyes became fixed on it, but not one asked me about it or asked the time. Then we began to avoid looking at each other and transferred our attentions to the vast open countryside and to the distant screen of date palms in the direction of the east that kept our vehicle company and hid the villages along the Shatt al-Arab.

We arrived at noon and someone showed me to the hotel which lies at the intersection of straight roads and looks on to a square in the middle of which is a round fenced garden. The hotel consisted of two low storeys, while the balcony that overlooked the square was at such a low height that someone in the street could have climbed up on to it. I, who cannot bear the smell of hotels, or the heavy, humid shade in their hallways in daytime, hastened to call out to its owners. When I repeated my call, a boy looked down from a door at the side and said: "Do you want to sleep here?"

"Have you a place?" I said.

The boy went into the room and from it there emerged a man whom I asked for a room with a balcony. The boy who was showing me the way informed me that the hotel would be empty by day and packed at night. Just as the stairway was the shortest of stairways and the balcony the lowest of balconies, my room was the smallest and contained a solitary bed, but the sun entered it from the balcony. I threw my bag on to the bed and the boy sat down beside me. "The doors are all without locks," said the boy. "Why should we lock them? – the travellers only stay for one night."

Then he leaned towards me and whispered: "Are you Indian?"

This idea came as a surprise to me. The boy himself was more likely to be Indian with his dark complexion, thick brilliantined hair, and sparkling eyes. I whispered to him: "Did they tell you that Basra used to be called the crotch of India, and that the Indian invaders in the British army, who came down to the land of Fao first of all, desired no other women except those of Basra?"

The boy ignored my cryptic reference to the mixing of passions and blending of races and asked, if I wasn't Indian, where did I live?

"I've come from Ashar," I told him, "on a visit to the watchmaker. Would you direct me to him?"

"Perhaps you mean the old man who has many clocks in his house," said the boy.

"Yes, that must be he," I said.

"He's not far from the hotel," he said. "He lives alone with his daughter and never leaves the house."

The boy brought us lunch from a restaurant, and we sat on the bed to eat, and he told me about the man I had seen downstairs: "He's not the owner of the hotel, just a permanent guest."

Then, with his mouth full of food, he whispered: "He's got a pistol."

"You know a lot of things, O Indian," I said, also speaking in a whisper.

He protested that he wasn't Indian but was from Hasa. He had a father who worked on the ships that transported dates from Basra to the coastal towns of the Gulf and India.

THE BOY took me to the watchmaker, leaving me in front of the door of his house. A gap made by a slab of stone that had been removed from its place in the upper frieze of the door made this entrance unforgettable. One day, in tropical years, there had stopped near where I was a sailor shaky with sickness, or some Sikh soldier shackled with lust, and he had looked at the slab of stone on which was engraved some date or phrase, before continuing on his unknown journey. And after those two there perhaps came some foreign archaeologist whose boat had been obstructed by the silt and who had put up in the town till the water rose, and his curiosity for things Eastern had been drawn to the curves of the writing on the slab of stone and he had torn it out and carried it off with him to his boat. Now I, likewise, was in front of this gateway to the sea.

On the boy's advice I did not hesitate to push open the door and enter into what looked like a porch which the sun penetrated through apertures near the ceiling and in which I was confronted by hidden and persistent ticking sounds and a garrulous ringing that issued from the pendulums and hammers of large clocks of the type that strike the hours, ranged along the two sides of the porch. As I proceeded one or more clocks struck at the same time. All the clocks were similar in size, in the great age of the wood of their frames, and in the shape of their round dials, their Roman numerals, and their delicate arrowlike hands – except that these hands were pointing to different times.

I had to follow the slight curve of the porch to come unexpectedly upon the last of the great sailors in his den, sitting behind a large table on which was heaped the wreckage of clocks. He was occupied with taking to pieces the movement of a clock by the light of a shaded lamp that hung down from the ceiling at a height close to his frail, white-haired head. He looked towards me with a glance from one eye that was naked and another on which a magnifying-glass had been fixed, then went back to disassembling the movement piece by piece. The short glance was sufficient to link this iron face with the nuts, cogwheels, and hands of the movements of the many clocks hanging on the walls and thrown into corners under dust and rust. Clocks that didn't work and others that did, the biggest of them being a clock on the wall above the watchmaker's head, which was, to be precise, the movement of a large grandfather clock made of brass, the dial of which had been removed and which had been divested of its cabinet so that time manifested itself in it naked and shining, sweeping along on its serrated cogwheels in a regular mechanical sequence: from the rotation of the spring to the pendulum that swung harmoniously to and fro and ended in the slow, tremulous, imperceptible movement of the hands. When the cogwheels had taken the hands along a set distance of time's journey, the striking cogwheel would move and raise the hammer. I had not previously seen a naked, throbbing clock and thus I became mesmerized by the regular throbbing that synchronized with the swinging motion of the pendulum and with the movement of the cogwheels of various diameters. I started at the sound of the hammer falling against the bell; the gallery rang with three strokes whose reverberations took a long time to die away, while the other clocks went on, behind the glass of their cabinets, with their incessant ticking.

The watchmaker raised his head and asked me if the large clock above his head had struck three times.

Then, immersing himself in taking the mechanism to pieces, he said: "Like horses; like horses running on the ocean bed."

A clock in the porch struck six times and he said: "Did one of them strike six times? It's six in America. They're getting up now, while the sun is setting in Burma."

Then the room was filled again with noisy reverberations. "Did it strike seven? It's nighttime in Indonesia. Did you make out the last twelve strokes? They are fast asleep in the furthest west of the world. After some hours the sun will rise in the furthest east. What time is it? Three? That's our time, here near the Gulf."

One clock began striking on its own. After a while the chimes blended with the tolling of other clocks as hammers coincided in falling upon bells, and others landed halfway between the times of striking and yet others fell between these halfways so that the chimes hurried in pursuit of one another in a confused scale. Then, one after another, the hammers became still, the chimes growing further apart, till a solitary clock remained, the last clock that had not discharged all its time, letting it trickle out now in a separate, high-pitched reverberation.

He was holding my watch in his grasp. "Several clocks might strike together," he said, "strike as the fancy takes them. I haven't liked to set my clocks to the same time. I have assigned to my daughter the task of merely winding them up. They compete with one another like horses. I have clocks that I bought from people who looted them from the houses of Turkish employees who left them as they hurried away after the fall of Basra. I also got hold of clocks that were left behind later on by the Jews who emigrated. Friends of mine, the skippers of ships, who would come to visit me here, would sell me clocks of European manufacture. Do you see the clock over there in the passageway? It was in the house of the Turkish commander of the garrison of Fao's fortress."

I saw the gleam of the quick-swinging pendulum behind glass in the darkness of the cabinets of the clocks in the porch. Then I asked him about my watch. "Your watch? It's a rare one. They're no longer made. I haven't handled such a watch for a long time. I'm not sure about it but I'll take it to pieces. Take a stroll round and come back here at night."

That was what I'd actually intended to do. I would return before night. The clocks bade me farewell with successive chimes. Four chimes in Fao: seven P.M. in the swarming streets of Calcutta. Four chimes: eight A.M. in the jungles of Buenos Aires . . . Outside the den the clamour had ceased, also the smell of engine oil and of old wood.

I RETURNED AT sunset. I had spent the time visiting the old barracks which had been the home of the British army of occupation, then I had sat in a café near the fish market.

I didn't find the watchmaker in his former place, but presently I noticed a huge empty cabinet that had been moved into a gap between the clocks. The watchmaker was in an open courtyard before an instrument made up of clay vessels, which I guessed to be a type of water-clock. When he saw me he called out: "Come here. Come, I'll show you something."

I approached the vessels hanging on a cross-beam: from them water dripped into a vessel hanging on another, lower cross-beam; the water then flowed on to a metal plate on the ground, in which there was a gauge for measuring the height of the water.

"A water-clock?"

"Have you seen one like it?"

"I've read about them. They were the invention of people of old."

"The Persians call them *bingan*."

"I don't believe it tells the right time."

"No, it doesn't, it reckons only twenty hours to the day. According to its reckoning I'm 108 years old instead of ninety, and it is seventy-eight years since the British entered Basra instead of sixty. I learned how to make it from a Muscati sailor who had one like it in his house on the coast."

I followed him to the den, turning to two closed doors in the small courtyard on which darkness had descended. He returned the empty clock-cabinet to its place and seated himself in his chair. His many clothes lessened his appearance of senility; he was lost under his garments, one over another and yet another over them, his head inside a vast tarbush.

"I've heard you spent a lifetime at sea."

"Yes. It's not surprising that our lives are always linked to water. I was on one of the British India ships as a syce with an English trader dealing in horses."

He toyed with the remnants of the watches in front of him, then said: "He used to call himself by an Arabic name. We would call him Surour Saheb. He used to buy Nejdi horses from the rural areas of the south and they would then be shipped to Bombay where they would be collected up and sent to the racecourses in

England. Fifteen days on end at sea, except that we would make stops at the Gulf ports. We would stop for some days in Muscat. When there were strong winds against us we would spend a month at sea. The captains, the cooks and the pilots were Indians, while the others, seamen and syces, were from Muscat, Hasa, and Bahrain; the rest were from the islands of the Indian Ocean. We would have with us divers from Kuwait. I remember their small dark bodies and plaited hair as they washed down the horses on the shore or led them to the ship. I was the youngest syce. I began my first sea journey at the age of twelve. I joined the ship with my father who was an assistant to the captain and responsible for looking after the stores and equipment. There were three of us, counting my father, who would sleep in the storeroom among the sacks and barrels of tar, the fish oil, ropes and dried fish, on beds made up of coconut fibre."

"Did you make a lot?"

"We? We didn't make much. The trader did. Each horse would fetch eight hundred rupees in Bombay, and when we had reached Bengal it would fetch fifteen hundreed rupees. On our return to Basra we would receive our wages for having looked after the horses. Some of us would buy goods from India and sell them on our return journey wherever we put in: cloth, spices, rice, sugar, perfumes, and wood, and sometimes peacocks and monkeys."

"Did you employ horses in the war?"

"I myself didn't take part in the war. Of course they used them. When the Turks prevented us from trading with them because they needed them for the army, we moved to the other side of the river. We had a corral and a caravanserai for sleeping in at Khorramshahr. From there we began to smuggle out the horses far from the clutches of the Turkish customs men. On the night when we'd be travelling we'd feed and water the horses well and at dawn we'd proceed to the corral and each syce would lead out his horse. As for me I was required to look after the transportation of the provisions and fodder; other boys who were slightly older than me were put in charge of the transportation of the water, the ropes, the chains, and other equipment. The corral was close to the shore, except that the horses would make a lot of noise and stir up dust when they were being pulled along by the reins to the ship that would lie at the end of an anchorage stretching out to it from the shore. The ship would rock and tiny bits of straw would become stuck on top of our heads while the syces would call the horses by their names, telling them to keep quiet, until they finished tying them up in their places. It was no easy matter, for during the journey the waves, or the calm of the invisible sea, would excite one of the horses or would make it ill, so that its syce would have to spend the night with it, watching over it and keeping it company. As we lay in our sleeping quarters we would hear the syce reassuring his horse with some such phrase as: "Calm down, Calm down, my Precious Love. The grass over there is better." However, this horse, whose name was Precious Love, died somewhere near Aden. At dawn the sailors took it up and consigned it to the waves. It was a misty morning and I was carrying a lantern, and I heard the great carcase hitting the water, though without seeing it; I did, though, see its syce's face close to me – he would be returning from his voyage without any earnings."

Two or three clocks happened to chime together. I said to him:

"Used you to put in to Muscat?"

"Yes. Did I tell you about our host in Muscat? His wooden house was on the shore of a small bay, opposite an old stone fortress on the other side. We would set out for his house by boat. By birth he was a highlander, coming from the tribes in the mountains facing the bay. He was also a sorcerer. He was a close friend of Surour Saheb, supplying him with a type of ointment the Muscati used to prepare out of mountain herbs, which the Englishman would no sooner smear on his face than it turned a dark green and would gleam in the lamplight like a wave among rocks. In exchange for this the Muscati would get tobacco from him. I didn't join them in smoking, but I was fond of chewing a type of olibanum that was to be found extensively in the markets of the coast. I would climb up into a high place in the room that had been made as a permanent bed and would watch them puffing out the smoke from the *narghiles* into the air as they lay relaxing round the fire, having removed their dagger-belts and placed them in front of them alongside their coloured turbans. Their beards would be plunged in the smoke and the rings would glitter in their ears under the combed locks of hair whenever they turned towards the merchant, lost in thought. The merchant, relaxing on feather cushions, would be wearing brightly coloured trousers of Indian cloth and would be wrapped round in an *aba* of Kashmir wool; as for his silk turban, he would, like the sailors, have placed it in front of him beside his pistol."

"Did you say that the Muscati was a sorcerer?"

"He had a basket of snakes in which he would lay one of the sailors, then bring him out alive. His sparse body would be swallowed in his lustrous flowing robes, as was his small head in his saffron-coloured turban with the tassels. We were appalled at his repulsive greed for food, for he would eat a whole basketful of dates during a night and would drink enough water to provide for ten horses. He was amazing, quite remarkable; he would perform bizarre acts; swallowing a puff from his *narghile*, he would after a while begin to release the smoke from his mouth and nose for five consecutive minutes. You should have seen his stony face, with the clouds of smoke floating against it like serpents that flew and danced. He was married to seven women for whom he had dug out, in the foot of the mountain, rooms that overlooked the bay. No modesty prevented him from disclosing their fabulous names: Mountain Flower, Daylight Sun, Sea Pearl, Morning Star. He was a storehouse of spicy stories and tales of strange travels and we would draw inspiration from him for names for our horses. At the end of the night he would leave us sleeping and would climb up the mountain. At the end of one of our trips we stayed as his guest for seven nights, during which time men from the Muscati's tribe visited us to have a smoke; they would talk very little and would look with distaste at the merchant and would then leave quietly with their antiquated rifles.

"Our supper would consist of spiced rice and grilled meat or fish. We would be given a sweet sherbet to drink in brass cups. As for the almond-filled *halva* of Muscat that melts in the mouth, even the bitter coffee could not disperse its scented taste. In the morning he would return and give us some sherbet to drink that would settle our stomachs, which would be suffering from the night's food and drink, and would disperse the tobacco fumes from the sailors' heads."

An outburst of striking clocks prevented him momentarily from enlarging further. He did not wait for the sound to stop before continuing:

"On the final night of our journey he overdid his tricks in quite a frightening manner. While the syces would seek help from his magic in treating their sick horses, they were afraid nonetheless that the evil effects of his magic would spread and reap the lives of these horses. And thus it was that a violent wind drove our ship on to a rock at the entrance to the bay and smashed it. Some of us escaped drowning, but the sorcerer of Muscat was not among them. He was travelling with the ship on his way to get married to a woman from Bombay; but the high waves choked his shrieks and eliminated his magic."

"And the horses?"

"They combated the waves desperately. They were swimming in the direction of the rocky shore, horses battling against the white horses of the waves. All of them were drowned. That was my last journey in the horse ships. After that, in the few years that preceded the war, I worked on the mail ships."

He made a great effort to remember and express himself:

"In Bahrain I married a woman who bore me three daughters whom I gave in marriage to sons of the sea. I stayed on there with the boatbuilders until after the war. Then, in the thirties, I returned to Basra and bought the clocks and settled in Fao, marrying a woman from here."

"You are one of the few sailors who are still alive today."

He asked me where I lived and I told him that I had put up at the hotel. He said:

"A friend of mine used to live in it. I don't know if he's still alive – for twenty years I haven't left my house."

Then, searching among the fragments of watches, he asked me in surprise:

"Did you come to Fao just because of the watch?"

I answered him that there were some towns one had to go to. He handed me my watch. It was working. Before placing it in my hand he scrutinized its flap on which had been engraved a ship with a triangular sail, which he said was of the type known as *sunbuk*.

I opened the flap. The hands were making their slow way round. The palms of my hand closed over the watch, and we listened to the sea echoing in the clocks of the den. The slender legs of horses run in the streets of the clock faces, are abducted in the glass of the large grandfather clocks. The clocks tick and strike: resounding hooves, chimes driven forward like waves. A chime: the friction of chains and ropes against wet wood. Two chimes: the dropping of the anchor into the blue abyss. Three: the call of the rocks. Four: the storm blowing up. Five: the neighing of the horses. Six...seven...eight...nine...ten...eleven... twelve...

THIS WINDING LANE is not large enough to allow a lorry to pass, but it lets in a heavy damp night and sailors leading their horses, and a man dizzy from seasickness, still holding in his

grasp a pocket watch and making an effort to avoid the water and
the gentle sloping of the lane and the way the walls curve round.
The bends increase with the thickening darkness and the silence.
Light seeps through from the coming bend, causing me to
quicken my step. In its seeping through and the might of its radi-
ation it seems to be marching against the wall, carving into the
damp brickwork folds of skins and crumpled faces that are the
masks of seamen and traders from different races who have
passed by here before me and are to be distinguished only by
their headgear: the bedouin of Nejd and the rural areas of the
south by the *kuffiyeh* and *'iqal*, the Iraqi effendis of the towns by
the *sidara*; the Persians by the black tarbooshes made of goat-
skin; the Ottoman officers, soldiers, and government employees
by their tasselled tarbooshes; the Indians by their red turbans;
the Jews by flat red tarbooshes; the monks and missionaries by
their black head coverings; the European sea captains by their
naval caps; the explorers in disguise. . . . They rushed out towards the rustling noise coming from behind the last bend, the
eerie rumbling, the bated restlessness of the waves below the
high balustrades. . . . Then, here are Fao's quays, the lamps
leading its wooden bridges along the water for a distance; in the
spaces between them boats are anchored one alongside another,
their lights swaying; there is also a freighter with its lights on,
anchored between the two middle berths. It was possible for me
to make out in the middle of the river scattered floating lights. I
didn't go very close to the quay installations but contented myself with standing in front of the dark, bare extension of the
river. To my surprise a man who was perhaps working as a
watchman or worker on the quays approached me and asked me
for the time. Eleven.

On my return to the hotel I took a different road, passing by
the closed shops. I was extremely alert. The light will be shining
brightly in the hotel vestibule. The oil stove will be in the middle
of it, and to one side of the vestibule will be baggage, suitcases, a

watercooling box, and a cupboard. Seated on the bench will be a man who is dozing, his cigarette forgotten between his fingers. It will happen that I shall approach the door of my room, shall open the door, and shall find him sleeping in my bed; he will be turned to the wall, having hung his red turban on the clothes hook.

Translated by DENYS JOHNSON-DAVIES

The Way of the Wind*

✳   ✳   ✳   ✳   ✳

Amos Oz was born in 1939 in Jerusalem, and is in-
ternationally celebrated for his fiction and nonfic-
tion, which explore the difficulties of life
in Israel.

1

*G*IDEON SHENHAV's last day began with a brilliant sunrise. The dawn was gentle, almost autumnal. Faint flashes of light flickered through the wall of cloud that sealed off the eastern horizon. Slyly the new day concealed its purpose, betraying no hint of the heat wave that lay enfolded in its bosom.

Purple glowed on the eastern heights, fanned by the morning breeze. Then the rays pierced through the wall of cloud. It was day. Dark loopholes blinked awake at daylight's touch. Finally the incandescent sphere rose, assaulted the mountains of cloud, and broke their ranks. The eastern horizon was adazzle. And the soft purple yielded and fled before the terrible crimson blaze.

The camp was shaken by reveille a few minutes before sunrise. Gideon rose, padded barefoot out of his hut, and, still asleep, looked at the gathering light. With one thin hand he shad-

---

*The Hebrew word *ruah* has multiple meanings: wind, spirit, intellect, ghost, to mention only a few. In this story it also refers to the ideological convictions of the old man. The title is borrowed from Ecclesiastes 11.5. –TRANS.

ed his eyes, still yearning for sleep, while the other automatically buttoned up his battle dress. He could already hear voices and metallic sounds; a few eager boys were cleaning their guns for morning inspection. But Gideon was slow. The sunrise had stirred a weary restlessness inside him, perhaps a vague longing. The sunrise was over, but still he stood there drowsily, until he was pushed from behind and told to get cracking.

He went back into the hut, straightened his camp bed, cleaned his submachine gun, and picked up his shaving kit. On his way, among whitewashed eucalyptus trees and clustering notices commending tidiness and discipline, he suddenly remembered that today was Independence Day, the Fifth of Iyar. And today the platoon was to mount a celebratory parachute display in the Valley of Jezreel. He entered the washroom and, while he waited for a free mirror, brushed his teeth and thought of pretty girls. In an hour and a half the preparations would be complete and the platoon would be airborne, on its way to its destination. Throngs of excited civilians would be waiting for them to jump, and the girls would be there, too. The drop would take place just outside Nof Harish, the kibbutz that was Gideon's home, where he had been born and brought up until the day he joined the army. The moment his feet touched the ground, the children of the kibbutz would close around him and jump all over him and shout, "Gideon, look, here's our Gideon!"

He pushed in between two much bigger soldiers and began to lather his face and try to shave.

"Hot day," he said.

One of the soldiers answered, "Not yet. But it soon will be."

And another soldier behind him grumbled, "Hurry it up. Don't spend all day jawing."

Gideon did not take offense. On the contrary, the words filled him with a surge of joy for some reason. He dried his face and went out onto the parade ground. The blue light had changed meanwhile to gray-white, the grubby glare of a *khamsin*.

2

SHIMSHON SHEINBAUM had confidently predicted the previous night that a *khamsin* was on its way. As soon as he got up he hurried over to the window and confirmed with calm satisfaction that he had been right yet again. He closed the shutters to protect the room from the hot wind, then washed his face and his shaggy shoulders and chest, shaved, and prepared his breakfast, coffee with a roll brought last night from the dining hall. Shimshon Sheinbaum loathed wasting time, especially in the productive morning hours: you go out, walk to the dining hall, have a chat, read the paper, discuss the news, and that's half the morning gone. So he always made do with a cup of coffee and a roll, and by ten past six, after the early news summary, Gideon Shenhav's father was sitting at his desk. Summer and winter alike, with no concessions.

He sat at his desk and stared for a few minutes at the map of the country that hung on the opposite wall. He was straining to recapture a nagging dream which had taken hold of him in the early hours, just before he had awakened. But it eluded him. Shimshon decided to get on with his work and not waste another minute. True, today was a holiday, but the best way to celebrate was to work, not to slack off. Before it was time to go out and watch the parachutists – and Gideon, who might actually be among them and not drop out at the last minute – he still had several hours of working time. A man of seventy-five cannot afford to squander his hours, especially if there are many, painfully many, things he must set down in writing. So little time.

THE NAME of Shimshon Sheinbaum needs no introduction. The Hebrew Labor Movement knows how to honor its founding fathers, and for decades now Shimshon Sheinbaum's name has been invested with a halo of enduring fame. For decades he has fought body and soul to realize the vision of his youth. Setbacks and disappointments have not shattered or weakened his faith but, rather, have enriched it with a vein of wise sadness. The better he has come to understand the weakness of others and their ideological deviations, the more ferociously he has fought against his own weaknesses. He has sternly eliminated them, and lived according to his principles, with a ruthless self-discipline and not without a certain secret joy.

At this moment, between six and seven o'clock on this Independence Day morning, Shimshon Sheinbaum is not yet a bereaved father. But his features are extraordinarily well suited to the role. A solemn, sagacious expression, of one who sees all but betrays no reaction, occupies his furrowed face. And his blue eyes express an ironic melancholy.

He sits erect at his desk, his head bent over the pages. His elbows are relaxed. The desk is made of plain wood, like the rest of the furniture, which is all functional and unembellished. More like a monastic cell than a bungalow in a long-established kibbutz.

This morning will not be particularly productive. Time and again his thoughts wander to the dream that flickered and died at the end of the night. He must recapture the dream, and then he will be able to forget it and concentrate on his work. There was a hose, yes, and some sort of goldfish or something. An argument with someone. No connection. Now to work. The Poalei Zion Movement appears to have been built from the start on an ideological contradiction that could never be bridged, and which it only succeeded in disguising by means of verbal acrobatics. But the contradiction is only apparent, and anyone who hopes to exploit it to undermine or attack the movement does not know what he is talking about. And here is the simple proof.

SHIMSHOM SHEINBAUM'S rich experience of life has taught

him how arbitrary, how senseless is the hand that guides the vagaries of our fate, that of the individual and that of the community alike. His sobriety has not robbed him of the straightforwardness which has animated him since his youth. His most remarkable and admirable characteristic is his stubborn innocence, like that of our pure, pious forebears, whose sagacity never injured their faith. Sheinbaum has never allowed his actions to be cut loose from his words. Even though some of the leaders of our movement have drifted into political careers and cut themselves off completely from manual labor, Sheinbaum has never abandoned the kibbutz. He has turned down all outside jobs and assignments, and it was only with extreme reluctance that he accepted nomination to the General Workers' Congress. Until a few years ago his days were divided equally between physical and intellectual work: three days gardening, three days theorizing. The beautiful gardens of Nof Harish are largely his handiwork. We can remember how he used to plant and prune and lop, water and hoe, manure, transplant, weed, and dig up. He did not permit his status as the leading thinker of the movement to exempt him from the duties to which every rank-and-file member is liable: he served as night watchman, took his turn in the kitchens, helped with the harvest. No shadow of a double standard has ever clouded the path of Shimshon Sheinbaum's life; he is a single complex of vision and execution, he has known no slackness or weakness of will – so the secretary of the movement wrote about him in a magazine a few years ago, on the occasion of his seventieth birthday.

True, there have been moments of stabbing despair. There have been moments of deep disgust. But Shimshon Sheinbaum knows how to transform such moments into secret sources of furious energy. Like the words of the marching song he loves, which always inspires him to a frenzy of action: *Up into the mountains we are climbing, Climbing up toward the dawning day; We have left all our yesterdays behind us, but tomorrow is a long long way away.* If only that stupid dream would emerge from the shadows and show itself clearly, he could kick it out of his mind and concentrate at last on his work. Time is slipping by. A rubber hose, a chess gambit, some goldfish, a great argument, but what is the connection?

FOR MANY YEARS Shimshon Sheinbaum has lived alone. He has channeled all his vigor into his ideological productions. To this life's work he has sacrificed the warmth of a family home. He has managed, in exchange, to retain into old age a youthful clarity and cordiality. Only when he was fifty-six did he suddenly marry Raya Greenspan and father Gideon, and after that he left her and returned to his ideological work. It would be sanctimonious to pretend, however, that before his marriage Shimshon Sheinbaum maintained a monastic existence. His personality attracted women just as it attracted disciples. He was still young when his thick mop of hair turned white, and his sunbeaten face was etched with an appealing pattern of lines and wrinkles. His square back, his strong shoulders, the timbre of his voice – always warm, skeptical, and rather ruminative – and also his solitude, all attracted women to him like fluttering birds. Gossip attributes to his loins at least one of the urchins of the kibbutz, and elsewhere, too, stories are current. But we shall not dwell on this.

At the age of fifty-six Shimshon Sheinbaum decided that it befitted him to beget a son and heir to bear his stamp and his name into the coming generation. And so he conquered Raya Greenspan, a diminutive girl with a stammer who was thirty-three years his junior. Three months after the wedding, which was solemnized before a restricted company, Gideon was born. And before the kibbutz had recovered from its amazement, Shimshon sent Raya back to her former room and rededicated

himself to his ideological work. This episode caused various rip-
ples, and, indeed, it was preceded by painful heart-searchings in
Shimshon Sheinbaum himself.

NOW LET'S CONCENTRATE and think logically. Yes, it's coming
back. She came to my room and called me to go there quickly to
put a stop to that scandal. I didn't ask any questions, but hurried
after her. Someone had had the nerve to dig a pond in the lawn in
front of the dining hall, and I was seething because no one had
authorized such an innovation, an ornamental pond in front of
the dining hall, like some Polish squire's château. I shouted.
Who at, there is no clear picture. There were goldfish in the
pond. And a boy was filling it with water from a black rubber
hose. So I decided to put a stop to the whole performance there
and then, but the boy wouldn't listen to me. I started walking
along the hose to find the faucet and cut off the water before any-
body managed to establish the pond as a *fait accompli*. I walked
and walked until I suddenly discovered that I was walking in a
circle, and the hose was not connected to a faucet but simply
came back to the pond and sucked up water from it. Stuff and
nonsense. That's the end of it. The original platform of the
Poalei Zion Movement must be understood without any re-
course to dialectics, it must be taken literally, word for word.

3

AFTER HIS SEPARATION from Raya Greenspan, Shimshon
Sheinbaum did not neglect his duties as his son's mentor, nor did
he disclaim responsibility. He lavished on him, from the time
the boy was six or seven, the full warmth of his personality. Gideon, however, turned out to be something of a disappointment,
not the stuff of which dynasties are founded. As a child he was always sniveling. He was a slow, bewildered child, mopping up

blows and insults without retaliating, a strange child, always playing with candy wrappers, dried leaves, silkworms. And from the age of twelve he was constantly having his heart broken by girls of all ages. He was always lovesick, and he published sad poems and cruel parodies in the children's newsletter. A dark, gentle youth, with an almost feminine beauty, who walked the paths of the kibbutz in obstinate silence. He did not shine at work; he did not shine in communal life. He was slow of speech and no doubt also of thought. His poems seemed to Shimshon incorrigibly sentimental, and his parodies venomous, without a trace of inspiration. The nickname Pinocchio suited him, there is no denying it. And the infuriating smiles he was perpetually spreading on his face seemed to Shimshon a depressingly exact replica of the smiles of Raya Greenspan.

And then, eighteen months before, Gideon had amazed his father. He suddenly appeared and asked for his written permission to enlist in the paratroopers – as an only son this required the written consent of both parents. Only when Shimshon Sheinbaum was convinced that this was not one of his son's outrageous jokes did he agree to give his consent. And then he gave it gladly: this was surely an encouraging turn in the boy's development. They'd make a man of him there. Let him go. Why not?

But Raya Greenspan's stubborn opposition raised an unexpected obstacle to Gideon's plan. No, she wouldn't sign the paper. On no account. Never.

Shimshon himself went to her room one evening, pleaded with her, reasoned with her, shouted at her. All in vain. She wouldn't sign. No reason, she just wouldn't. So Shimshon Sheinbaum had to resort to devious means to enable the boy to enlist. He wrote a private letter to Yolek himself, asking a personal favor. He wished his son to be allowed to volunteer. The mother was emotionally unstable. The boy would make a first-rate paratrooper. Shimshon himself accepted full responsibility.

And incidentally, he had never before asked a personal favor. And he never would again. This was the one and only time in his whole life. He begged Yolek to see what he could do.

At the end of September, when the first signs of autumn were appearing in the orchards, Gideon Shenhav was enrolled in a parachute unit.

FROM THAT TIME ON, Shimshon Sheinbaum immersed himself more deeply than ever in ideological work, which is the only real mark a man can leave on the world. Shimshon Sheinbaum has made a mark on the Hebrew Labor Movement that can never be erased. Old age is still far off. At seventy-five he still has hair as thick as ever, and his muscles are firm and powerful. His eyes are alert, his mind attentive. His strong, dry, slightly cracked voice still works wonders on women of all ages. His bearing is restrained, his manner modest. Needless to say, he is deeply rooted in the soil of Nof Harish. He loathes assemblies and formal ceremonies, not to mention commissions and official appointments. With his pen alone he has inscribed his name on the roll of honor of our movement and our nation.

4

GIDEON SHENHAV'S last day began with a brilliant sunrise. He felt he could even see the beads of dew evaporating in the heat. Omens blazed on the mountain peaks far away to the east. This was a day of celebration, a celebration of independence and a celebration of parachuting over the familiar fields of home. All that night he had nestled in a half-dream of dark autumnal forests under northern skies, a rich smell of autumn, huge trees he could not name. All night long pale leaves had been dropping on the huts of the camp. Even after he had awakened in the morning, the northern forest with its nameless trees still continued to whisper in his ears.

Gideon adored the delicious moment of free fall between the jump from the aircraft and the unfolding of the parachute. The void rushes up toward you at lightening speed, fierce drafts of air lick at your body, making you dizzy with pleasure. The speed is drunken, reckless, it whistles and roars and your whole body trembles to it, red-hot needles work at your nerve ends, and your heart pounds. Suddenly, when you are lightning in the wind, the chute opens. The straps check your fall, like a firm, masculine arm bringing you calmly under control. You can feel its supporting strength under your armpits. The reckless thrill gives way to a more sedate pleasure. Slowly your body swings through the air, floats, hesitates, drifts a little way on the slight breeze, you can never guess precisely where your feet will touch ground, on the slope of that hill or next to the orange groves over there, and like an exhausted migrating bird you slowly descend, seeing roofs, roads, crows in the meadow, slowly as if you have a choice, as if the decision is entirely yours.

And then the ground is under your feet, and you launch into the practiced somersault which will soften the impact of landing. Within seconds you must sober up. The coursing blood slows down. Dimensions return to normal. Only a weary pride survives in your heart until you rejoin your commanding officer and your comrades and you're caught up in the rhythm of frenzied reorganization.

THIS TIME it is all going to happen over Nof Harish.

The older folk will raise their clammy hands, push back their caps, and try to spot Gideon among the gray dots dangling in the sky. The kids will rush around in the fields, also waiting excitedly for their hero to touch down. Mother will come out of the dining hall and stand peering upward, muttering to herself. Shimshon will leave his desk for a while, perhaps take a chair out onto his little porch and watch the whole performance with pensive pride.

Then the kibbutz will entertain the unit. Pitchers of lemonade glistening with chilly perspiration will be set out in the dining hall, there will be crates of apples, or perhaps cakes baked by the older women, iced with congratulatory phrases.

By six-thirty the sun had grown out of its colorful caprice and risen ruthlessly over the eastern mountain heights. A thick heat weighed heavily on the whole scene. The tin roofs of the camp huts reflected a dazzling glare. The walls began to radiate a dense, oppressive warmth into the huts. On the main road, which passed close to the perimeter fence, a lively procession of buses and trucks was already in motion: the residents of the villages and small towns were streaming to the big city to watch the military parade. Their white shirts could be discerned dimly through the clouds of dust, and snatches of exuberant song could be caught in the distance.

The paratroopers had completed their morning inspection. The orders of the day, signed by the Chief of Staff, had been read out and posted on the bulletin boards. A festive breakfast had been served, including a hard-boiled egg reposing on a lettuce leaf ringed with olives.

Gideon, his dark hair flopping forward onto his forehead, broke into a quiet song. The others joined him. Here and there someone altered the words, making them comical or even obscene. Soon the Hebrew songs gave way to a guttural, almost desperate Arabic wail. The platoon commander, a blond, good-looking officer whose exploits were feted around the campfires at night, stood up and said: "That's enough." The paratroopers stopped singing, hastily downed the last of their greasy coffee, and moved toward the runways. Here there was another inspection; the commanding officer spoke a few words of endearment to his men, calling them "the salt of the earth," and then ordered them into the waiting aircraft.

The squadron commanders stood at the doors of the planes and checked each belt and harness. The CO himself circulated

among the men, patting a shoulder, joking, predicting, enthus-
ing, for all the world as though they were going into battle and
facing real danger. Gideon responded to the pat on his shoulder
with a hasty smile. He was lean, almost ascetic-looking, but very
suntanned. A sharp eye, that of the legendary blond commander, could spot the blue vein throbbing in his neck.

Then the heat broke into the shady storage sheds, mercilessly
flushing out the last strongholds of coolness, roasting everything
with a gray glow. The sign was given. The engines gave a throaty
roar. Birds fled from the runway. The planes shuddered, moved
forward heavily, and began to gather the momentum without
which takeoff cannot be achieved.

5

I MUST GET OUT and be there to shake his hand.

Having made up his mind, Sheinbaum closed his notebook.
The months of military training have certainly toughened the
boy. It is hard to believe, but it certainly looks as though he is beginning to mature at last. He still has to learn how to handle
women. He has to free himself once and for all from his shyness
and his sentimentality: he should leave such traits to women and
cultivate toughness in himself. And how he has improved at
chess. Soon he'll be a serious challenge to his old father. May
even beat me one of these days. Not just yet, though. As long as
he doesn't up and marry the first girl who gives herself to him.
He ought to break one or two of them in before he gets spliced.
In a few years he'll have to give me some grandchildren. Lots of
them. Gideon's children will have two fathers: my son can take
care of them, and I'll take care of their ideas. The second generation grew up in the shadow of our achievements; that's why
they're so confused. It's a matter of dialectics. But the third generation will be a wonderful synthesis, a successful outcome: they
will inherit the spontaneity of their parents and the spirit of their

grandparents. It will be a glorious heritage distilled from a twisted pedigree. I'd better jot that phrase down, it will come in handy one of these days. I feel so sad when I think of Gideon and his friends: they exude such an air of shallow despair, of nihilism, of cynical mockery. They can't love wholeheartedly, and they can't hate wholeheartedly, either. No enthusiasm, and no loathing. I'm not one to deprecate despair per se. Despair is the eternal twin of faith, but that's real despair, virile and passionate, not this sentimental, poetic melancholy. Sit still, Gideon, stop scratching yourself, stop biting your nails. I want to read you a marvelous passage from Brenner. All right, make a face. So I won't read. Go outside and grow up to be a Bedouin, if that's what you want. But if you don't get to know Brenner, you'll never understand the first thing about despair or about faith. You won't find any soppy poems here about jackals caught in traps or flowers in the autumn. In Brenner everything is on fire. Love, and hatred as well. Maybe you yourselves won't see light and darkness face to face, but your children will. A glorious heritage will be distilled from a twisted pedigree. And we won't let the third generation be pampered and corrupted by sentimental verses by decadent poetesses. Here come the planes now. We'll put Brenner back on the shelf and get ready to be proud of you for a change, Gideon Sheinbaum.

6

SHEINBAUM STRODE purposefully across the lawn, stepped up onto the concrete path, and turned toward the plowed field in the southwest corner of the kibbutz, which had been selected for the landing. On his way he paused now and again at a flower bed to pull up a stray weed skulking furtively beneath a flowering shrub. His small blue eyes had always been amazingly skillful at detecting weeds. Admittedly, because of his age he had retired a few years previously from his work in the gardens, but until his dying day he would not cease to scan the flower beds mercilessly in search of undesirable intruders. At such moments he thought of the boy, forty years his junior, who had succeeded him as gardener and who fancied himself as the local watercolorist. He had inherited beautifully tended gardens, and now they were all going to seed before our very eyes.

A gang of excited children ran across his path. They were fiercely absorbed in a detailed argument about the types of aircraft that were circling above the valley. Because they were running, the argument was being carried out in loud shouts and gasps. Shimshon seized one of them by the shirttail, forcibly brought him to a halt, put his face close to the child's, and said:

"You are Zaki."

"Leave me alone," the child replied.

Sheinbaum said: "What's all this shouting? Airplanes, is that all you've got in your heads? And running across the flower beds like that where it says Keep Off, is that right? Do you think you can do whatever you like? Are there no rules any more? Look at me when I'm speaking to you. And give me a proper answer, or..."

But Zaki had taken advantage of the flood of words to wriggle out of the man's grasp and tear himself free. He slipped in among the bushes, made a monkey face, and stuck out his tongue.

Sheinbaum pursed his lips. He thought for an instant about old age, but instantly thrust it out of his mind and said to himself: All right. We'll see about that later. Zaki, otherwise Azariah. Rapid calculation showed that he must be at least eleven, perhaps twelve already. A hooligan. A wild beast.

Meanwhile the young trainees had occupied a vantage point high up on top of the water tower, from which they could survey the length and breadth of the valley. The whole scene reminded Sheinbaum of a Russian painting. For a moment he was tempted to climb up and join the youngsters on top of the tower, to watch the display comfortably from a distance. But the thought of the

manly handshake to come kept him striding steadily on, till he
reached the edge of the field. Here he stood, his legs planted well
apart, his arms folded on his chest, his thick white hair falling
impressively over his forehead. He craned his neck and followed
the two transport planes with steady gray eyes. The mosaic of
wrinkles on his face enriched his expression with a rare blend of
pride, thoughtfulness, and a trace of well-controlled irony. And
his bushy white eyebrows suggested a saint in a Russian icon.
Meanwhile the planes had completed their first circuit, and the
leading one was approaching the field again.

Shimshon Sheinbaum's lips parted and made way for a low
hum. An old Russian tune was throbbing in his chest. The first
batch of men emerged from the opening in the plane's side.
Small dark shapes were dotted in space, like seeds scattered by a
farmer in an old pioneering print.

Then Raya Greenspan stuck her head out of the window of the
kitchen and gesticulated with the ladle she was holding as though
admonishing the treetops. Her face was hot and flushed. Perspiration stuck her plain dress to her strong, hairy legs. She panted,
scratched at her disheveled hair with the fingernails of her free
hand, and suddenly turned and shouted to the other women
working in the kitchens:

"Quick! Come to the window! It's Gidi up there! Gidi in the
sky!"

And just as suddenly she was struck dumb.

While the first soldiers were still floating gently, like a handful
of feathers, between heaven and earth, the second plane came in
and dropped Gideon Shenhav's group. The men stood pressed
close together inside the hatch, chest against back, their bodies
fused into a single tense, sweating mass. When Gideon's turn
came he gritted his teeth, braced his knees, and leapt out as
though from the womb into the bright hot air. A long wild
scream of joy burst from his throat as he fell. He could see his
childhood haunts rushing up toward him as he fell. He could see

the roofs and treetops and he smiled a frantic smile of greeting as he fell toward the vineyards and concrete paths and sheds and gleaming pipes with joy in his heart as he fell. Never in his whole life had he known such overwhelming, spine-tingling love. All his muscles were tensed, and gushing thrills burst in his stomach and up his spine to the roots of his hair. He screamed for love like a madman, his fingernails almost drawing blood from his clenched palms. Then the straps drew taut and caught him under the armpits. His waist was clasped in a tight embrace. For a moment he felt as though an invisible hand were pulling him back up toward the plane into the heart of the sky. The delicious falling sensation was replaced by a slow, gentle swaying, like rocking in a cradle or floating in warm water. Suddenly a wild panic hit him. How will they recognize me down there. How will they manage to identify their only son in this forest of white parachutes. How will they be able to fix me and me alone with their anxious, loving gaze. Mother and Dad and the pretty girls and the little kids and everyone. I musn't just get lost in the crowd. After all, this is me, and I'm the one they love.

That moment an idea flashed through Gideon's mind. He put his hand up to his shoulder and pulled the cord to release the spare chute, the one intended for emergencies. As the second canopy opened overhead he slowed down as though the force of gravity had lost its hold on him. He seemed to be floating alone in the void, like a gull or a lonely cloud. The last of his comrades had landed in the soft earth and were folding up their parachutes. Gideon Shenhav alone continued to hover as though under a spell with two large canopies spread out above him. Happy, intoxicated, he drank in the hundreds of eyes fixed on him. On him alone. In his glorious isolation.

As though to lend further splendor to the spectacle, a strong, almost cool breeze burst from the west, plowing through the hot air, playing with the spectators' hair, and carrying slightly eastward the last of the parachutists.

7

FAR AWAY in the big city, the massed crowds waiting for the military parade greeted the sudden sea breeze with a sigh of relief. Perhaps it marked the end of the heat wave. A cool, salty smell caressed the baking streets. The breeze freshened. It whistled fiercely in the treetops, bent the stiff spines of the cypresses, ruffled the hair of the pines, raised eddies of dust, and blurred the scene for the spectators at the parachute display. Regally, like a huge solitary bird, Gideon Shenhav was carried eastward toward the main road.

The terrified shout that broke simultaneously from a hundred throats could not reach the boy. Singing aloud in an ecstatic trance, he continued to sway slowly toward the main electric cables, stretched between their enormous pylons. The watchers stared in horror at the suspended soldier and the powerlines that crossed the valley with unfaltering straightness from west to east. The five parallel cables, sagging with their own weight between the pylons, hummed softly in the gusty breeze.

Gideon's two parachutes tangled in the upper cable. A moment later his feet landed on the lower one. His body hung backward in a slanting pose. The straps held his waist and shoulders fast, preventing him from falling into the soft plowland. Had he not been insulated by the thick soles of his boots, the boy would have been struck dead at the moment of impact. As it was, the cable was already protesting its unwonted burden by scorching his soles. Tiny sparks flashed and crackled under Gideon's feet. He held tight with both hands to the buckles on the straps. His eyes were open wide and his mouth was agape.

Immediately a short officer, perspiring heavily, leapt out of the petrified crowd and shouted:

"Don't touch the cables, Gidi. Stretch your body backward and keep as clear as you can!"

The whole tightly packed, panic-stricken crowd began to edge slowly in an easterly direction. There were shouts. There was a wail. Sheinbaum silenced them with his metallic voice and ordered everyone to keep calm. He broke into a fast run, his feet pounding on the soft earth, reached the spot, pushed aside the officers and curious bystanders, and instructed his son:

"Quickly, Gideon, release the straps and drop. The ground is soft here. It's perfectly safe. Jump."

"I can't."

"Don't argue. Do as I tell you. Jump."

"I can't, Dad, I can't do it."

"No such thing as can't. Release the straps and jump before you electrocute yourself."

"I can't, the straps are tangled. Tell them to switch off the current quickly, Dad, my boots are burning."

Some of the soldiers were trying to hold back the crowd, discourage well-meaning suggestions, and make more room under the powerlines. They kept repeating, as if it were an incantation, "Don't panic please don't panic."

The youngsters of the kibbutz were rushing all around, adding to the confusion. Reprimands and warnings had no effect. Two angry paratroopers managed to catch Zaki, who was idiotically climbing the nearest pylon, snorting and whistling and making faces to attract the attention of the crowd.

The short officer suddenly shouted: "Your knife. You've got a knife in your belt. Get it out and cut the straps!"

But Gideon either could not or would not hear. He began to sob aloud.

"Get me down, Dad, I'll be electrocuted, tell them to get me down from here, I can't get down on my own."

"Stop sniveling," his father said curtly. "You've been told to use your knife to cut the straps. Now, do as you've been told. And stop sniveling."

The boy obeyed. He was still sobbing audibly, but he groped for the knife, located it, and cut the straps one by one. The silence was total. Only Gideon's sobbing, a strange, piercing sound, was to be heard intermittently. Finally one last strap was left holding him, which he did not dare to cut.

"Cut it," the children shrilled, "cut it and jump. Let's see you do it."

And Shimshon added in a level voice, "Now what are you waiting for?"

"I can't do it," Gideon pleaded.

"Of course you can," said his father.

"The current," the boy wept. "I can feel the current. Get me down quickly."

His father's eyes filled with blood as he roared:

"You coward! You ought to be ashamed of yourself!"

"But I can't do it, I'll break my neck, it's too high."

"You can do it and you must do it. You're a fool, that's what you are, a fool and a coward."

A GROUP OF JET PLANES passed overhead on their way to the aerial display over the city. They were flying in precise formation, thundering westward like a pack of wild dogs. As the planes disappeared, the silence seemed twice as intense. Even the boy had stopped crying. He let the knife fall to the ground. The blade pierced the ground at Shimshon Sheinbaum's feet.

"What did you do that for?" the short officer shouted.

"I didn't mean it," Gideon whined. "It just slipped out of my hand."

Shimshon Sheinbaum bent down, picked up a small stone, straightened up, and threw it furiously at his son's back.

"Pinocchio, you're a wet rag, you're a miserable coward!"

At this point the sea breeze also dropped.

The heat wave returned with renewed vigor to oppress both men and inanimate objects. A red-haired, freckled soldier muttered to himself, "He's scared to jump, the idiot, he'll kill himself if he stays up there." And a skinny, plain-faced girl, hearing this, rushed into the middle of the circle and spread her arms wide:

"Jump into my arms, Gidi, you'll be all right."

"It would be interesting," remarked a veteran pioneer in working clothes, "to know whether anyone has had the sense to phone the electric company to ask them to switch off the current." He turned and started off toward the kibbutz buildings. He was striding quickly, angrily, up the slight slope when he was suddenly alarmed by a prolonged burst of firing close at hand. For a moment he imagined he was being shot at from behind. But at once he realized what was happening: the squadron commander, the good-looking blond hero, was trying to sever the electric cables with his machine gun.

Without success.

Meanwhile, a beaten-up truck arrived from the farmyard. Ladders were unloaded from it, followed by the elderly doctor, and finally a stretcher.

At that moment it was evident that Gideon had been struck by a sudden decision. Kicking out strongly, he pushed himself off the lower cable, which was emitting blue sparks, turned a somersault, and remained suspended by the single strap with his head pointing downward and his scorched boots beating the air a foot or so from the cable.

It was hard to be certain, but it looked as though so far he had not sustained any serious injury. He swung limply upside down in space, like a dead lamb suspended from a butcher's hook.

This spectacle provoked hysterical glee in the watching children. They barked with laughter. Zaki slapped his knees, choking and heaving convulsively. He leapt up and down screeching like a mischievous monkey.

What had Gideon Shenhav seen that made him suddenly stretch his neck and join in the children's laughter? Perhaps his peculiar posture had unbalanced his mind. His face was blood-red, his tongue protruded, his thick hair hung down, and only his feet kicked up at the sky.

8

A SECOND GROUP OF JETS plowed through the sky overhead. A dozen metallic birds, sculpted with cruel beauty, flashing dazzlingly in the bright sunlight. They flew in a narrow spearhead formation. Their fury shook the earth. On they flew to the west, and a deep silence followed.

Meanwhile, the elderly doctor sat down on the stretcher, lit a cigarette, blinked vaguely at the people, the soldiers, the scampering chidren, and said to himself: We'll see how things turn out. Whatever has to happen will happen. How hot it is today.

Every now and again Gideon let out another senseless laugh. His legs were flailing, describing clumsy circles in the dusty air. The blood had drained from his inverted limbs and was gathering in his head. His eyes were beginning to bulge. The world was turning dark. Instead of the crimson glow, purple spots were dancing before his eyes. He stuck his tongue out. The children interpreted this as a gesture of derision. "Upside-down Pinocchio," Zaki shrilled, "why don't you stop squinting at us, and try walking on your hands instead?"

Sheinbaum moved to hit the brat, but the blow landed on thin air because the child had leapt aside. The old man beckoned to the blond commander, and they held a brief consultation. The boy was in no immediate danger, because he was not in direct contact with the cable, but he must be rescued soon. This comedy could not go on forever. A ladder would not help much: he was too high up. Perhaps the knife could be got up to him again somehow, and he could be persuaded to cut the last strap and jump into a sheet of canvas. After all, it was a perfectly routine exercise in parachute training. The main thing was to act quickly, because the situation was humiliating. Not to mention the children. So the short officer removed his shirt and wrapped a knife in it. Gideon stretched his hands downward and tried to catch the bundle. It slipped between his outstretched arms and plummeted uselessly to the ground. The children snickered. Only after two more unsuccessful attempts did Gideon manage to grasp the shirt and remove the knife. His fingers were numb and heavy with blood. Suddenly he pressed the blade to his burning cheek, enjoying the cool touch of the steel. It was a delicious moment. He opened his eyes and saw an inverted world. Everything looked comical: the truck, the field, his father, the army, the kids, and even the knife in his hand. He made a twisted face at the gang of children, gave a deep laugh, and waved at them with the knife. He tried to say something. If only they could see themselves from up here, upside down, rushing around like startled ants, they would surely laugh with him. But the laugh turned into a heavy cough; Gideon choked and his eyes filled.

9

GIDEON'S UPSIDE-DOWN ANTICS filled Zaki with demonic glee.

"He's crying," he shouted cruelly, "Gideon's crying, look, you can see the tears. Pinocchio the hero, he's snivelling with fear-o. We can see you, we can."

Once again Shimshon Sheinbaum's fist fell ineffectually on thin air.

"Zaki," Gideon managed to shout in a dull, pain-racked voice, "I'll kill you, I'll choke you, you little bastard." Suddenly he chuckled and stopped.

It was no good. He wouldn't cut the last strap by himself, and the doctor was afraid that if he stayed as he was much longer he was likely to lose consciousness. Some other solution would have to be found. This performance could not be allowed to go on all day.

And so the kibbutz truck rumbled across the plowland and braked at the point indicated by Shimshon Sheinbaum. Two ladders were hastily lashed together to reach the required height, and then supported on the back of the truck by five strong pairs of hands. The legendary blond officer started to climb. But when he reached the place where the two ladders overlapped, there was an ominous creak, and the wood began to bend with the weight and the height. The officer, a largish man, hesitated for a moment. He decided to retreat and fasten the ladders together more securely. He climbed down to the floor of the truck, wiped the sweat from his forehead, and said, "Wait, I'm thinking." Just then, in the twinkling of an eye, before he could be stopped, the child Zaki had climbed high up the ladder, past the join, and leapt like a frantic monkey up onto the topmost rungs; suddenly he was clutching a knife – where on earth had he got it from? He wrestled with the taut strap. The spectators held their breath: he seemed to be defying gravity, not holding on, not caring, hopping on the top rung, nimble, lithe, amazingly efficient.

10

THE HEAT BEAT DOWN violently on the hanging youth. His eyes were growing dimmer. His breathing had almost stopped. With his last glimmer of lucidity he saw his ugly brother in front of him and felt his breath on his face. He could smell him. He could see the pointed teeth protruding from Zaki's mouth. A terrible fear closed in on him, as though he were looking in a mirror and seeing a monster. The nightmare roused Gideon's last reserves of strength. He kicked into space, flailed, managed to turn over, seized the strap, and pulled himself up. With outstretched arms he threw himself onto the cable and saw the flash. The hot wind continued to tyrannize the whole valley. And a third cluster of jets drowned the scene with its roaring.

11

THE STATUS of a bereaved father invests a man with a saintly aura of suffering. But Sheinbaum gave no thought to this aura. A stunned, silent company escorted him toward the dining hall. He knew, with utter certainty, that his place now was beside Raya.

On the way he saw the child Zaki, glowing, breathless, a hero. Surrounded by other youngsters: he had almost rescued Gideon. Shimshon laid a trembling hand on the child's head, and tried to tell him. His voice abandoned him and his lips quivered. Clumsily he stroked the tousled, dusty mop of hair. It was the first time he had ever stroked the child. A few steps later, everything went dark and the old man collapsed in a flower bed.

As Independence Day drew to a close the *khamsin* abated. A fresh sea breeze soothed the steaming walls. There was a heavy fall of dew on the lawns in the night.

What does the pale ring around the moon portend? Usually it heralds a *khamsin*. Tomorrow, no doubt, the heat will return. It is May, and June will follow. A wind drifts among the cypresses in the night, trying to comfort them between one heat wave and the next. It is the way of the wind to come and to go and to come again. There is nothing new.

Translated by NICHOLAS DE LANGE

Telephone Call

✳   ✳   ✳   ✳   ✳

Alifa Rifaat spent most of her adult life in different
parts of the Egyptian countryside, and draws much
of the material for her stories from those years. She
now lives in Cairo with her three children.

*F*ROM A NEARBY FLAT a telephone rings and rings, then
stops, and the number is redialled and the ringing starts again,
then stops, then starts again. What desperate contact is someone
trying to make at this hour of the night? Is it a matter of life or
death, or perhaps one of love? There is nothing like love to in-
duce such a state of despair, no other reason to explain such obstinacy: a lover has been left and seeks the opportunity to plead
to be allowed back. He must know that his beloved is at the other
end and is refusing to pick up the receiver.

   And here I am sitting for hours alone in my flat, knowing there
is no one to ring, that there is no question of pleading or submitting to any terms, for there is no way of communicating from the
grave. Does not everyone try to find some glimmer of hope even
in the darkest situations? Does not the man standing on the scaf-
fold hope that some miracle will, in the few seconds left, save
him? Is not history full of such miracles? And yet I don't really
ask for a miracle, nothing as tangible as that, just the very smallest of signs that he is there beyond the grave waiting for me. A
small sign that I would understand and I would seek nothing fur-

ther after that. Why, for instance, couldn't the vase of artificial flowers change its place from the small table by the window and I wake from sleep to find it on top of the bookcase? It is so little to ask.

The telephone has stopped ringing. Has the caller accepted his fate? Or has he sought temporary peace in sleep? It's late. The black head of night is being streaked with grey. These next few hours are the only ones during which Cairo knows a short period of quiet, a time when even the solitary cars that are about don't find it necessary to hoot. Outside the window the street is deserted except for the few cats that scavenge in peace at night and snatch their hours of sleep in the daytime.

Soon the call to dawn prayers will float like clouds of sound across the sleeping city. I shall hear it from three different mosques that surround our building. The calls will follow one another not quite synchronized, so that when one is pronouncing the *shahadah*[1], another will be telling me that "prayer is better than sleep" – I who spend my nights awake.

The night around me is pregnant with a silence that speaks of memories. The familiar objects tell me of the life I lived so fully and which, with his death, has come to a sudden stop. Since then I have been waiting. Otherwise, what is the significance of the forty days after death? Has it not come down to us from the Pharaohs, those experts on death, that during these days the dead are still hovering around us and only later take themselves off elsewhere? If he is to communicate, then it must surely be during this period, for after that we shall truly be in two separate worlds.

I must try to stop myself from thinking of the terrible changes being wrought on that face and body I loved so much. How often had I prayed that I might die first and be spared the struggle to continue in life without him.

1. The doctrinal formula in Islam.

As usual I am waiting for the call to dawn prayers, after which I shall go to my bedroom and sleep for a few hours. The maid will let herself into the flat with her own key, clean up, bring in the necessities for life and put them in the fridge, take the money I leave for her, and depart. This is the only way to live at present, to turn life upside down, to sleep, with the aid of sleeping pills, during the hours when life is being led, and to be awake with my thoughts of him when the world around me is sleeping: to turn life upside down and thus to be partly dead to it.

The silence is torn apart by the ringing of the telephone. Ever since he died the telephone has been silent, except perhaps during the day when the maid would answer and tell the caller that her mistress was not available and did not want any calls. But who would ring at such an hour? As the noise bored into my ears I suddenly knew the significance of the call. No, it would not be his voice at the other end; things were done more subtly than that. I knew exactly what would happen.

I walked towards the little side table, the one we'd bought together, and with a steady hand raised the receiver to my ear. As I had expected, no voice broke the silence. I held it closer to my ear, thinking that maybe there would be the sound of breathing, but even this I told myself would not happen. What was happening demanded a high degree of faith on my part. Life and death were both a matter of faith. As I held the receiver tightly against my ear it was as though, like the Sufi image of the water taking on the colour of its container, I were being poured from a container of black despair into one of light-filled hope and confidence. And so I sat holding a soundless receiver to my ear for what might have been minutes or hours. In such circumstances, what is time? Then, suddenly, the spell was broken and the line went dead. I woke from my reverie to the first words of the call to prayer seeping through into the room.

I rose and made my ablutions, then returned to the living room, spread out my prayer carpet and performed the dawn prayer. As I sat with my prayer-beads, I was conscious of being enveloped in a cloak of contentment and gratitude. I knew for certain that all was right.

The all-pervading silence was shattered by the ringing of the telephone again, more blaring and insistent than the first time. I tried to will it to stop, for I felt an instinctive reluctance to answer it. After sitting for so long with my prayer-beads, my legs were stiff and shook with exhaustion as I walked across the room to the telephone. In trepidation I picked up the receiver and the voice of the operator immediately greeted me:

"Good morning, madam. I'm sorry for the call you had some minutes ago. It was a call from abroad and the call was put through to you by mistake. Please accept our apologies for waking you at this hour."

"It doesn't matter," I said and replaced the receiver.

I went back and sat down again on the prayer carpet. My hand was trembling as the prayer-beads ran through my fingers and I kept on asking pardon of the Almighty. Only now I was aware of the enormity of what I had sought from Him and which, in my simplicity, I had thought He had granted: a sign from the beyond. Then I was reminded of how when the Prophet, on whom be the blessings and peace of God, died, the Muslims were plunged into consternation and disbelief by the news and of Abu Bakr's words to them: "For those of you who worship Muhammed, Muhammed is dead; and for those who worship Allah, Allah is alive and dies not."

Though the tears were running down my cheeks, I finally felt at peace with myself in submitting to what the Almighty had decreed.

Translated by D E N Y S J O H N S O N - D A V I E S

V

A Glorious Morning, Comrade

✳   ✳   ✳   ✳   ✳

Maurice Gee was born in 1933 in New Zealand and
has written novels, children's books, screenplays,
and teleplays. He has won a number of literary
awards in his native country.

*M*ERCY TIED her father's scarf in a mean granny knot.

"Now remember, darling, if you want the little house just
bang on the wall. We don't want any wets with the girls all here."
And Barbie, gentler, but not to be outdone, knelt and zipped up
his slippers. "You'll be lovely and warm in the sun, won't you?
Just bang on the wall. No little accidents please. 'Bye daddums."

They left him in his rocking chair on the veranda and he
rocked a little, pitying their innocence. He did not mean to pee in
his pants today. He had other plans.

Presently the "girls" came, driving their little cars; and they
walked up the path in twos and threes, dumpy women or stringy,
the lot, in Saturday clothes and coloured hair. They stopped for
a little chat of course, politely, and sniffed behind their hands to
see if he had behaved himself today. They were good-hearted
women. Mercy and Barbie attracted such.

"Lucky you, Mr. Pitt-Rimmer. Just loafing in the sun."

He counted them. Ten. Three tables. There was Madge Og-
den, a daughter of divorcees; and Pearl Edwards who taught
mathematics at the Girls' High School; and Mary Rendt who

had wanted to be a nun but had lost her faith and married a German Christian Scientist and lost that faith and her husband too; and the three Bailey girls, with not a husband amongst them, whose mother had broken their hearts by choosing to live in an old people's home; and Christine Hunt who had been caught shoplifting when she was a girl and lived it down and married the son of the mayor; and Jean Murray-Briggs, whose name annoyed him; and last the lesbians, though none of the others knew – Phyllis Wedderburn and Margaret Way. Charles Pitt-Rimmer, he knew. He winked at them and they blushed, but seemed a little pleased.

"Such lovely sun. We've only got old bridge."

He gave them time to get warmed up. Mercy looked out once and wagged her finger, and Barbie once and kissed him on the cheek.

They would forget him when they were well ahead. His daughters were the top pair in the district and he wished he could feel more pleased with them for it.

When the time came he stood up and walked along the veranda. He went down the path, down the steps, along the footpath to the park, and into the trees. It was twenty-nine minutes past two. He had run away twice before. Today he would outfox them. He would keep away from roads and butcher shops, where he had been caught twice before looking at roasts of beef. They would not think of searching on the hill.

Girls, he wrote in his mind, *There are other things than meat. Your father played chess.*

At nineteen minutes to three he reached the dairy. "Here you children, out of my way," he said, and they stood aside with a quickness that pleased him. He did not mind that they giggled. That was proper in children.

"A bag of Turkish delight," he said. He had planned it all morning and it came out with an English sound. "And a packet of cigarettes."

The woman behind the counter had a half-witted face, a nose that seemed to snuffle for scent like a dog's. She gave a smile and said, "It's Mr. Pitt-Rimmer, isn't it?"

"My name is not your concern. Turkish delight. And a packet of cigarettes."

"Sit down, Mr. Pitt-Rimmer. There's a chair right there. As soon as I've served these kiddies I'll ring Mrs. Parsloe."

"You will not ring Mrs. Parsley. I wish to be served. Am I a customer or am I not? And are you in business? Answer me that."

He was pleased to see confusion in her eyes. "I'll have de Reszke."

"Whosie?"

"De Reszke. You don't seem to know your business, madam. Do you make a living? I wonder at it."

"There's nothing here called de Reszke."

"Cigarettes. Cigarettes. Named after a great operatic tenor. Before your time, of course. I understand. It's all Bing Crosby today."

The woman went suddenly to the telephone. "You kiddies wait." She started to dial.

"Very well," cried Charles Pitt-Rimmer. "You may ring Mrs. Parsley. Tell her I'm striking out. I have my life. Tell her I'm smoking again. De Reszke. And eating Turkish delight." He stopped at the door. "And if she wishes to know where I am you may say that I've gone to the butcher's for a piece of German sausage."

"Mrs. Parsloe?" the woman said. "It's the Regal dairy. Your father's here."

He was very pleased with himself as he turned up the hill. Capablanca would have been proud of that move.

Girls, bridge is for simple folk. You must think ahead. I've never cared for German sausage.

He looked at his watch. It was thirteen minutes to three. Already he had beaten his old record. He pictured the little cars scuttling about Hardinge, driven in a dangerous manner by women with blue and pink hair. Barbie would be crying – he was sorry about that – and Mercy with her eye like a hanging judge's.

Girls, a man's a man for a' that.

He followed a path into the trees and climbed until he stood on the edge of the cliff with the wharves below him. Three minutes past three. He would have liked some Turkish delight. He had not had any since his last day in court, which was twenty-two years ago. His secretary used to bring in a paper bag full with his lunch. The gob-stopper he'd taken from the Regal dairy's counter would be no substitute. But he found that he enjoyed it once he'd torn the paper off. It tasted of raspberry, a flavour he'd forgotten.

He went to the safety fence and looked down. A girl had jumped down there on Boxing Day because her employer, a well-known man in Hardinge, had put her in the family way. She had lived for two hours but not said a word. He had heard Mercy and Barbie discussing it, in voices hushed but full of glee and dread. The man, Barbie said, was "a weed in the garden of life" – which she'd pinched from her mother, who had also believed that such men should be hanged. Women had a poor understanding of certain needs.

The gob-stopper made him feel bilious. He put it in his pocket. Below him ships were tied up at the wharves, all piddling water out of their sides. One of them was a phosphate tub, moored at a wharf that he remembered now was Pitt-Rimmer Wharf. There had been those years on the Harbour Board – a tedious business. Jack Hunt had picked his nose behind the agenda. The Hunts had never been up to much though they liked to believe that they were the bosses of Hardinge. He walked on and the cape came into sight, standing up like Chunuk Bair. He had no wish to be reminded of that. That had been a very great piece of nonsense.

Girls, you persist in reminding me . . . .

A woman came towards him leading a tiny black dog in a tartan jacket.

"I don't care for dogs, madam. Keep him off."

"Mr. Pitt-Rimmer. Don't you remember me?"

"I've met many people. Fifteen thousand is my calculation."

"But I'm Maisie Transome. Maisie Jack that was. You used to give me lollies."

"Your mother was an excellent secretary. And a kindly soul. She had extraordinary bosoms."

"Ooh, Mr. Pitt-Rimmer, you're a rogue."

"I don't care for animals sniffing about my feet."

"Come here, Bruce. Where are your manners, darling? Mr. Pitt-Rimmer, can I walk home with you? You shouldn't be out you know, dressed like that. Barbie told me you're being very naughty."

"My daughter has more kindness than sense. She's a good woman but she's had a tragic life."

"Who? Barbie?"

"She fell in love with a young man in my office. Parsley was his name. Mercy stole him away. 'Mercy' was not my choice. I want that understood. My wife had a poor grip on reality. But Parsley – she married him and broke her sister's heart. Barbie never married. Parsley was not a good catch, mind you. She was well out of it. He played around as they say. There was a woman in my office called Rona Jack. Her marriage was unsatisfactory. Parsley used to visit there."

"Oh, Mr. Pitt-Rimmer –"

"He died of course. They nursed him. My daughters are good girls."

"But my parents had an ideal marriage. They were in love till the day they died."

"Indeed. I congratulate them. You should not speak with strangers. The risks are very great. Good day to you."

"But I'm taking you home, remember?"

"I wish to relieve myself."

She did not follow him though her dog yapped in an impertinent way. The path led downhill and had many troublesome curves. His legs began to be sore. But a bank of nasturtiums pleased him and a smell of fennel. Fennel made him think of aniseed balls. He stopped at the memory. When sucked an aniseed ball turned white. And Turkish delight left sugar round the mouth.

Girls, when you were children I bought you sweets. Straps of licorice. Be fair. Bags of sherbet. Bags of chocolate fudge.

The path ended by the Salvation Army Eventide Home. Two old men were sitting on a bench. "A glorious morning, comrade," one of them said.

"Glorious," Charles Pitt-Rimmer agreed, smiling at his better knowledge. It was twenty-nine minutes past three in the afternoon and his daughters were thoroughly bamboozled. He stopped by the reservoir and sat down on a bank. A boy was walking along a pipe, and a smaller boy rode up on a tricycle.

"Why are you wearing your dressing gown?"

"Old men are allowed to."

"Mummy makes me get dressed. Have you wet your pants?"

"I believe I have."

"Couldn't you find a toilet? You could use ours."

"The word is lavatory. You should not be frightened of calling things by their names."

"Mummy said lavatory's not nice."

"And you should not pay too much attention to women."

Charles Pitt-Rimmer dozed for a moment. "Poor Parsley. They made him eat his vegetable. Curly kale. A weed."

"Mummy makes me eat my vegetables."

"What do you have for pudding?"

His mind was lucid about food but cloudy about everything

else. He was not quite sure where he was. "My favourite is lemon meringue pie." He felt in his pocket for the gob-stopper and gave it to the child who put it in his mouth at once, leaving only the stick poking out.

"You speak too much of your mother. The conspiracy starts at the cradle."

The boy who had been walking on the pipe ran up to join them.

"Give us a lick, Tony. Come on."

Charles Pitt-Rimmer went to sleep. He believed he was in a bath of lukewarm water that was turning cold about his legs. Soon he was wakened by a woman's voice.

"Let me see that. Give it to me at once. It's filthy. It's got a hair on it."

She moved her arm violently and the boy on the tricycle cried. Charles did not know what was happening, but he saw that the woman was looking at him with hatred and was astonished at the ease with which people felt this emotion. Forty years of court work had not got him used to it.

"Beware, madam. It can get to be a habit."

"You ought to be ashamed of yourself. And you" – she rounded on the older boy – "I told you to look after him. Why can't you listen for once? Get into the washhouse and wait till your father comes home."

Now the older boy cried. They were an emotional family and seemed to be without reason, Charles decided. They vanished and he was relieved. He lay on the bank and tried to sleep, curled into a ball to defeat the cold. Where were his daughters? Where were the wretched women?

Girls, you're selfish creatures....

Again a woman woke him. This time it was Christine Hunt, with her hair like candy floss. He reached out for some.

"What are you doing? Oh! Mr. Pitt-Rimmer. Let go."

"Christine Perkins, you were lucky to get off with a fine. If you hadn't had me to conduct your defence you would have gone to prison."

"Oh! Oh! My hair. You've ruined it."

"Why did you choose such frilly things, Christine? If you remember, I told the court they were for your glory box? A clever touch. But you can tell me. I can be discreet."

"You're a horrible man. Oh, look, you've wet your pyjamas. This is dreadful."

"I understand, Christine. It's difficult to be poor. No nice frillies, eh? A girl likes frillies. But I always believed you married beneath you. Your father-in-law picks his nose."

"My father-in-law has been dead for twenty years. And you've ruined our afternoon. You know that, don't you? It's a wonder to me how Mercy and Barbie keep going. They must be saints."

"They're vegetarians. They struggle to ward off despair. I do my best."

"Mr. Pitt-Rimmer, I'm going to take you home. I am. Now come with me. Come on."

She put out her hand and he was appalled at the size of it. It went right round his wrist, and her silver nails poked up from the underside. She was appalled too. She jerked away.

"Barbie will be the invalid when I'm dead," said Charles Pitt-Rimmer.

Christine Hunt went away. "I'm going to get your daughters. Don't you move." Her little car scuttled off, and Charles lay curled up tightly.

Girls, it's time for my nap. You're selfish creatures....

"Oh daddums, daddums, why do you do these things?"

"Put down the rubber sheet, Barbie. No, spread it out, you ninny."

They put him in the back seat and Barbie sat with him, rubbing his hands.

"You're so naughty, so naughty –"

"I've had enough," Mercy cried. "I'm going to put you in a home. You've made a fool of me for the last time. Wipe his mouth, Barbie, can't you see?"

"You make it so hard for us, daddums. Oh, your hands are so cold."

"I walked on the pipe, Mercy. If I'd fallen off you would never have been born."

They washed him and put him to bed. He slept smiling for two hours, then rang his bell for tea. They propped him up with pillows, and Barbie sat with him while he ate.

"It's a special salad, daddums. One Mercy found. It's got avocados in it. Now drink your apple juice."

She took away the tray and came back with his library book.

"Promise me you won't be naughty again. It makes us so sad."

"What was the time when you caught me?"

"Four o'clock. You were gone for two hours. Oh daddums –"

"An hour and thirty-one minutes." He grinned at her.

When she had gone he finished his book. He corrected one split infinitive and underlined two mentions of female breasts. Then he made his secret sign on page eighty-eight.

Barbie was doing the dishes and Mercy watching a television show full of American voices. On the final page, below a scene of love, Charles wrote a message:

My daughters are keeping me prisoner. Help! I have not had a piece of meat for twenty years. . . .

Pear Tree Dance

✳   ✳   ✳   ✳   ✳

Elizabeth Jolley was born in England in 1923 and
moved to Australia in 1959 with her husband and
three children. She is the author of several novels including *Miss Peabody's Inheritance* and
Mr. Scobie's Riddle.

No ONE KNEW where the Newspaper of Claremont Street
went in her spare time.

Newspaper, or Weekly as she was called by those who knew
her, earned her living by cleaning other people's houses. There
was something she wanted to do more than anything else, and for
this she needed money. For a long time she had been saving, putting money aside in little amounts. Every morning, when she
woke up, she thought about her money. The growing sum
danced before her, growing a little more. She calculated what
she would be able to put in the bank. She was not very quick at
arithmetic. As she lay in bed she used the sky as a blackboard,
and in her mind, wrote the figures on the clouds. The total sum
came out somewhere halfway down her window.

While she was working in the different houses she sang, "*the
bells of hell go ting a ling a ling for you and not for me.*" She liked
hymns best.

"Well 'ow are we?" she called out when she went in in the
mornings. "Ow's everybody today?" And she would throw open

windows and start pulling the stove to pieces. She knew every-thing about all the people she cleaned for and she never missed anything that was going on.

"I think that word should be clay – C-L-A-Y." She helped old Mr. Kingston with his crossword puzzle.

"Chattam's girl's engaged at long larst," she reported to the Kingstons. "Two rooms full of presents, yo' should just see!"

"Kingston's boy's 'ad 'orrible accident," she described the de-tails to the Chathams. "Lorst 'is job first, pore boy! Pore Mrs. Kingston!" Weekly sadly shook the tablecloth over the floor and carried out some dead roses carefully as if to keep them for the next funeral.

"*I could not do without Thee Thou Saviour of the Lorst,*" she sang at the Butterworths.

She cleaned in all sorts of houses. Her body was hard like a board and withered with so much work she seemed to have stopped looking like a woman.

On her way home from work she always went in the little shop at the end of Claremont Street and bought a few things, taking her time and seeing who was there and watching what they bought.

"Here's the Newspaper of Claremont Street," the two shop girls nudged each other.

"Any pigs been eating babies lately, Newspaper?" one of them called out.

"What happened to the man who sawed off all his fingers at the timber mill?" the other girl called. "You never finished telling us."

No one needed to read anything, the Newspaper of Claremont Street told them all the news.

One Tuesday afternoon when she had finished her work, she went to look at the valley for the first time. All the morning she was thinking about the long drive. She wondered which would be the shortest way to get to this place hidden behind the pastures and foothills along the South West Highway. It was a strain thinking about it and talking gossip at the same time, especially as she kept thinking too that she had no right really to go looking at land.

All land is somebody's land. For Weekly the thought of possessing some seemed more of an impertinence than a possibility. Perhaps this was because she had spent her childhood in a slaty backyard where nothing would grow except thin carrots and a few sunflowers. All round the place where she lived the slag heaps smouldered and hot cinders fell on the paths. The children gathered to play in a little thicket of stunted thornbushes and elderberry trees. There were patches of coltsfoot and they picked the yellow flowers eagerly till none was left. Back home in the Black Country where it was all coal mines and brick kilns and iron foundries her family had never had a house or a garden. Weekly had nothing behind her not even the place where she was born. It no longer existed. As soon as she was old enough she was sent into service. Later she left her country with the family where she was employed. All her life she had done domestic work. She was neat and quick and clean and her hands were rough like nutmeg graters and she knew all there was to know about people and their ways of living.

Weekly lived in a rented room, it was covered with brown linoleum which she polished. The house was built a long time ago for a large family but now the house was all divided up. Every room had a different life in it and every life was isolated from all the other lives.

Except for the old car she bought, Weekly, the Newspaper of Claremont Street, had no possessions. Nothing in the room belonged to her except some old books and papers, collected and hoarded, and her few washed-out and mended clothes. She lived quite alone and, when she came home tired after her long day of work, she took some bread and boiled vegetables from the fly-screen cupboard where she kept her food, and she sat reading and eating hungrily. She was so thin and her neck so scraggy that, when she swallowed, you could see the food going down. But as she had no one there to see and to tell her about it, it did not really matter. While it was still light, Weekly pulled her chair across to the narrow window of her room and sat bent over her mending. She darned everything. She put on patches with a herringbone stitch. Sometimes she made the worn out materials of her skirts firmer with rows of herringboning, one row neatly above the other, the brown thread glowing in those last rays of the sun which make all browns beautiful. Even the old linoleum could have a sudden richness at this time of the evening. It was like the quick lighting up of a plain girl's face when she smiles because of some unexpected happiness.

It was when she was driving out to the country on Sundays in her old car she began to wish for some land, nothing very big, just a few acres. She drove about and stared into green paddocks fenced with round poles for horses and scattered in the corners with red flame-tree flowers and splashed all over with white lilies. She stopped to admire almond blossom and she wished for a little weatherboard house, warm in the sun, fragrant with orange trees and surrounded by vines. Sometimes she sat for hours alone in the scrub of a partly cleared piece of bush and stared at the few remaining tall trees, wondering at their age, and at the yellow tufts of Prickly Moses surviving.

The advertisements describing land for sale made her so excited she could hardly read them. As soon as she read one she became so restless she wanted to go off at once to have a look.

"Yo' should 'ave seen the mess after the Venns' party," she called to Mrs. Lacey. "Broken glass everywhere, blood on the stairs, and a whole pile of half-eaten pizzas in the laundry. Some people think they're having a good time! And you'll never believe this, I picked up a bed jacket, ever so pretty it was, to wash it and, would you believe, there was a yuman arm in it. . . ." The Newspaper of Claremont Street talked all the time in the places where she worked. It was not for nothing she was called Newspaper or Weekly, but all the time she was talking she never spoke about the land. Secretly she read her advertisements and secretly she went off to look.

She first went to the valley on a Tuesday after work.

"Tell about Sophie Whiteman," Diana Lacey tried to detain Weekly. Mrs. Lacey had, as usual, gone to town and Diana was in bed with a sore throat.

"Wash the curtains, please," Mrs. Lacey felt this was a precaution against more illness. "We must get rid of the nasty germs," she said. "And Weekly, I think the dining-room curtains need a bit of sewing, if you have time, thank you," and she had rushed off late for the hairdresser.

"Well," said Weekly putting away the ironing board. "She got a pair of scissors and she went into the garding and she looked all about her to see no one was watching and she cut up a earthworm into a whole lot of little pieces."

"What did her mother do?" asked Diana joyfully, knowing from a previous telling.

"Well," said Weekly, "she came in from town and took orf her hat and her lovely fur coat, very beautiful lady, Mrs. Whiteman, she took orf her good clothes and she took Sophie Whiteman and laid her across her lap and give her a good hidin'."

"Oh!" Diana was pleased. "Was that before she died of the chocolate lining in her stomach or after?"

"Diana Lacey, what have I told you before, remember? Sophie Whiteman had her good hidin' afore she died. How could she cut up a worm after she died. Use yor brains!"

Weekly was impatient to leave to find the way to the valley. She found a piece of paper and scrawled a note for Mrs. Lacey.

"Will come early tomorrow to run up yor curtings W."

She knew she had to cross the Medulla brook and turn left at the twenty-nine mile peg. She found the valley all right.

After the turnoff, the road bends and climbs and then there it is, pasture on either side of the road with cattle grazing, straying towards a three-cornered dam. And, on that first day, there was a newly born calf which seemed unable to get up.

She saw the weatherboard house and she went up there and knocked.

"Excuse me, but can yo' tell me what part of the land's for sale?" her voice trembled.

The young woman, the tenant's wife, came out.

"It's all for sale," she said. They walked side by side.

"All up there," the young woman pointed to the hillside where it was steep and covered with dead trees and rocks and pigsties made from old railway sleepers and corrugated iron. Beyond was the light and shade of the sun shining through the jarrah trees.

"And down there," she flung her plump arm towards the meadow which lay smiling below.

"There's a few orange trees, neglected," she explained. "That in the middle is an apricot. That over there is a pear tree. And where you see them white lilies, that's where there's an old well. Seven acres this side."

They walked back towards the house.

"The pasture's leased just now," the young woman said. "But it's all for sale too, thirty acres and there's another eighteen in the scrub."

Weekly wanted to stay looking at the valley but she was afraid that the young woman would not believe she really wanted to buy some of it. She drove home in a golden tranquillity dreaming of her land embroidered with pear blossom and bulging with plump apricots. Her crooked feet were wet from the long weeds and yellow daisies of the damp meadow. The road turned and dropped. Below was the great plain. The neat ribs of the vineyards chased each other towards the vague outlines of the city. Beyond was a thin line shining like the rim of a china saucer. It was the sea, brimming, joining the earth to the sky.

While she scrubbed and cleaned she thought about the land

and what she would grow there. At night she studied pamphlets on fruit growing. She had enough money saved to buy a piece of land but she still felt she had no right.

Every Sunday she went out to look at the valley and every time she found something fresh. Once she noticed that on one side of the road was a whole long hedge of white wild roses. Another time it seemed as if sheep were on the hillside among the pigsties, but, when she climbed up, she saw it was only the light on some greyish bushes making them look like a quiet flock of sheep.

One evening she sat in the shop in Claremont Street, sucking in her cheeks and peering into other people's shopping bags.

"Last week yo' bought flour," she said to a woman.

"So what if I did?"

"Well you'll not be needing any terday," Weekly advised. "Now eggs yo' didn't get, yo'll be needing them!..."

"Pore Mr. Kingston," Weekly shook her head and addressed the shop. "I done 'is puzzle today. Mr. Kingston I said let me do your crossword – I doubt he'll leave his bed again."

Silence fell among the groceries and the women who were shopping. The silence remained unbroken for Weekly had forgotten to talk. She had slipped into thinking about the valley. All her savings were not enough, not even for a part of the meadow. She was trying to get over the terrible disappointment she had just had.

"If you're prepared to go out say forty miles," Mr. Rusk, the land agent, had said gently, "there's a nice five acres with a tin shack for tools. Some of it's river flats, suitable for pears. That would be within your price range." Mr. Rusk spoke seriously to the old woman even though he was not sure whether she was all right in the head. "Think it over," he advised. He always regarded a customer as a buyer until the customer did not buy.

Weekly tried to forget the valley, she began to scatter the new land with pear blossom. She would go at the weekend.

"Good night all!" She left the shop abruptly without telling any news at all.

On Sunday Weekly went to look at the five acres. It was more lovely than she had expected, and fragrant. A great many tall trees had been left standing and the tin shack turned out to be a tiny weatherboard cottage. She was afraid she had come to the wrong place.

"It must be someone's home," she thought to herself as she peered timidly through the cottage window and saw that it was full of furniture. Disappointment crept over her. Purple pig face was growing everywhere and, from the high verandah, she looked across the narrow valley to a hay field between big trees. There was such a stillness that Weekly felt more than ever that she was trespassing, not only on the land, but into the very depths of the stillness itself.

Mr. Rusk said that it was the five acres he had meant.

"I've never been there myself," he explained when she told him about the cottage. "Everything's included in the price."

Buying land takes time but Weekly contained herself in silence and patience, working hard all the days.

She began to buy things, a spade, rubber boots, some candles and groceries and polish and she packed them into the old car. Last of all she bought a pear tree, it looked so wizened she wondered how it could ever grow. Carefully she wrapped it in wet newspapers and laid it like a thin baby along the back seat.

On the day Mr. Rusk gave her the key, Weekly went to work with it pinned inside her dress. She felt it against her ribs all morning and in the afternoon she drove out to her piece of land.

The same trees and fragrance and the cottage were all there as before. This time she noticed honeysuckle and roses, a fig tree and a hedge of rosemary all neglected now and waiting for her to continue what some other person had started many years ago.

She thought she would die there that first day as she opened the cottage door to look inside. She looked shyly at the tiny rooms and wandered about on the land looking at it and breathing the warm fragrance. The noise of the magpies poured into the stillness and she could hear the creek, in flood, running. She sank down on to the earth as if she would never get up from it again. She counted over the treasures of the cottage. After having nothing she seemed now to have everything, a bed, table, chairs and in the kitchen, a wood stove and two toasting forks, a kettle and five flat irons. There was a painted cupboard too and someone had made curtains of pale-blue stuff patterned with roses.

Weekly wanted to clean out the cottage at once. She felt suddenly too tired. She rested on the earth and looked about her feeling the earth with her hands and listening as if she expected some great wisdom to come to her from the quiet trees and the undergrowth of the bush.

At about five o'clock the sun, before falling into the scrub, flooded the slope from the west and reddened the white bark of the trees. The sky deepened with the coming evening. Weekly forced her crooked old feet into the new rubber boots. She took the spade and the thin pear tree and went down to the mud flats at the bottom of her land.

Choosing a place for the pear tree she dug a hole. It was harder to dig in the clay than she thought it would be and she had to pause to rest several times.

She carried some dark earth from under a fallen tree over to the hole. Carefully she held the little tree in position and scattered the dark soft earth round the roots. She shook the little tree and scattered in more earth and then she firmed the soil, treading gently round and round the tree.

For the first time in her life the Newspaper of Claremont Street, or Weekly as she was called, was dancing. Stepping round and round the little tree she imagined herself to be like a bride dancing with lacy white blossom cascading on all sides.

Round and round the tree, dancing, firming the softly yielding earth with her new boots. And from the little foil label blowing in the restlessness of the evening came a fragile music for the pear tree dance.

VI

MARGARETA EKSTRÖM

Lilies of the Valley

✳   ✳   ✳   ✳   ✳

Margareta Ekström is a novelist, short story writer,
and poet, and the winner of many literary awards in
Sweden. Her work has been described by Susan
Sontag as "sensuous, beautifully felt, and truthful."
She has two books available in English, *The Day I
Began My Studies in Philosophy* and
Death's Midwives.

I . . . I . . . I . . .

Her hands grope over the bedding as though it were a keyboard. Blue-veined, swollen. Hard to make out the melody. The
room is so small and so filled with her smells. Medications. Old
age.

A whole room, walls lined with cheeses. When she saw them:
He! He's the right man! So many big round cheeses, and her
eyes as big as saucers. Provisions for the future. The flat. And
everything ready. The smell of cheese, betrothal and security.

Birds fly by the window. She raises her hand with difficulty.
Directs their flight in a trembling curve. Then they're gone.

The window regards her coolly and with clear eyes. Newly
washed by tears. Or sun? Again and again heavy machines fall
down across the sky. But when their noise sweeps through the
room she doesn't know from where it comes. Startled, she calls
out. But too softly. Emptiness.

She sleeps and she wakes. Whole cities pass. And villages with their wealth buried in the soil. The window shade a movie screen in the dark. Why do they keep it down? I'm awake. No, it is night.

Easy to get lost in the alleys of the night. Home: the fun place. The meadow where the accordions came out by midsummer, and finicky Kristina made her choke with laughter with her funny way of saying things. She said ... choked with laughter. Rolled around in the grass, got her face full of it.

You sure are a mess, girl! Reproaches shattered the Sunday harmony.

She'd just laughed. About her skirt, green from the grass. She'd twisted it around, and she had giggled and whispered. Finicky-Kristina. She could drive you crazy!

In the alleys of the night.

She'd never thought Stockholm was so big. Nor so confusing. They were both mirror and shield for each other. No nonsense allowed. The smallest of spots was examined and condemned ... their judgment was hard and regulations were as unyielding as hair pulled hard and straight into a bun. Their principles were like knotty wooden floors, worn smooth and scrubbed shining clean. Scrubbed so much that their tender skin was worn away, baring the very knuckles of their clear consciences.

How the waves glittered and tooted. The boats glared with their wet sides. Their flanks. Their bellies full of fish. Capable fingers pinch and press small dimples into the pieces of fish flesh. No one can deceive her. And the mistress will be pleased.

Long nights sleeping with her head on the kitchen table. Dishes done and silver already polished. But the cardplayers inside stay on and on. Belching smoke like a steamer. The heavy gate-key lies iron-cold on the table next to her sleeping brow. Kerchief's on and the table's as clean-scrubbed as the floor. Soon she'll hear the master's voice through the double doors. The last of the guests is to be shown down and let out. Not before she finally goes to sleep does the key stop swinging and come to rest on its hook.

Herring, smoked salmon, and split open eels. Hungrily and hoarsely the boats shriek for more to fill their empty metal bellies. The shores of Lake Malaren are full of poor, starving landowners ordering barrels full of herring, wheels of cheese, butter, and brandy. Do they want to eat us out of house and home?

And the alleys are teeming with little, dark men, running to fill the white bellies of the sea monsters with profusion from the stores.

It is good to own a shop like that.

How fast she walks! In spite of the cobblestones and the sun in her eyes. Walks fast? Not now. Sarcasm cuts off her recollections. Her feet are white now, like those of a princess. But she is expecting a black and imperious knight who has little interest in feet.

So fast she walks, her mind resumes obstinately. In a shower of winks and banter. Hesitating, she stops a while, fingering her purse and shopping list.

So strong they are, those chapped red hands. Her knuckles blanch and her thumbs sink into the oily mass of the cheeses as she lifts them. But her eyes twinkle and laughter flies about the marketplace like a sun-ray reflected by a moving mirror.

Herring brine has parched her hands. Looks as though she is wearing red working gloves. Beyond them her skin is lady-white.

"IS SHE SLEEPING?"

A wary smile passes over her lips.

The dark alley attracted her. Madame Mansson, queen of the Old Town. Madame Fortuna in person.

There is excitement in the air long before you reach that street. She is wandering there again now, her feet cool as linen sheets.

Chilly in the alleys between the houses. As though leftover

winter fog lay forgotten in the deepest recesses of July.

Where the street begins, the figure of a policeman. Face red like a sausage. Should investigate what those women are doing. But scared by the daring of his own thoughts, he makes an about-face, and piercing a sun-ray with the spike of his helmet, he disappears toward the marketplace.

She stands there in the chattering crowd of shady individuals. Is afraid of catching lice. Purses her lips so she looks like finicky Kristina. Nothing out and nothing in. But it is very tempting to relieve the torment of her anxiety by talking.

Her sparse eyebrows come together in an expression of anguish: "Is she in pain?"

It did hurt, in the end. Standing there, jammed on the cold porch. It had burned like blushing, deep into her soul, to yield to such temptation.

Like a group of high and inaccessible cypresses, a party of society ladies towered above the crowd. If they could, they'd have their fortunes told with their gloves on. I wonder whether that wouldn't be too much even for Madame Mansson?

The window-recesses were two meters deep and a couple of women with broad behinds were always jammed in them, out of breath and complaining about painful shoes and painful lives.

Suddenly she became aware of the purling trickle between the clogs and high-heeled boots. The hollows of the uneven cobblestones turn quickly into small yellow lagoons. Little by little, the trickle makes its way down the steps. A miniature torrent splashes around the ferrule of a parasol. Amused, she wonders whether the woman holding its handle in her mauve silk glove suspects what is taking place between her highly distinguished kid slippers. The anarchy of pantlessness is being proclaimed there.

I didn't find out my fortune, Finicky-Kristina. What? Don't you believe in the Mansson woman? No, I don't. She lied to me. You can't tell yet, you know. You'll find out by and by.

No, she lied. I could feel it here inside.

And she beats her chest so that the whale bones rattle in her corset. An awful noise. Cars as high up as the sky. Jet planes. In the newspaper you can read about when they crash and get killed. But who is this?

"Princess Birgitta."

This is Princess Birgitta?

"It is an advertisement for stockings, Grandmother."

Read what it says!

"You will never feel as elegant as when you wear Libido's spider-web crepe-nylon. . . ."

Crap-nylon!

"He follows your legs with glances that caress. . . ."

Yes, he'd like that, wouldn't he! That'd suit him just fine! Skirts are to go down to the ankle bones!

They lay and peeked at us through the reeds when we were bathing. But that was innocent. Showing your ankles was worse. . . for goodness sakes, how short your skirt is, lass.

To think that my daughter should wear her skirt that short!

"But Grandmother, I'm Sven's daughter, you're skipping a generation!"

What are you talking about? Didn't I recognize you? I guess I thought you were Martha. You do look like her.

So many they were. Could fill the whole Old Town. Where did they all come from? And she'd pressed her lips together so hard. Nothing out. No one in. But they pushed their way through, their heads bumpy like sacks of potatoes. It hurt terribly. Took several days sometimes. But that was one's punishment for committing an ugly sin, I suppose. The original sin.

But still it's a peculiar system. To have to hurt that much! Hard to really like someone who's hurt one so much. But then, they couldn't help it, the little creatures. Did look down upon them a little anyway for being so small. Had to help them grow.

Just like the man. So puny and wrinkled like a newborn. She had to help him grow. Like a child in her hands. In spite of his hurting her so.

My God, how you can dream!

Haven't done a thing for three whole days, I think.

"Three years, Grandmother dear. But don't worry about it!"

Three years! What are you saying, girl? To think that my own daughter should say a thing like that to me!

"Grandmother, I'm not Martha!"

She reaches carefully, oh, so carefully, because the body is treacherous nowadays, and a little movement turns suddenly into a violent gesture that upsets coffee cups and flower vases. A firm grasp with all five fingers relaxes unexpectedly to a helplessness that lets the water glass slide straight down onto the blanket. As though there were no hand at all, but instead a withered leaf hanging from a pain-wasted branch of arm.

But oh, so carefully now. Toward her crocheting. Which is bumpy and full of runs. Maybe it's the pattern? No, it isn't, she can see that now. The yarn is matted from her sweaty hands. Must be her very first crocheting in primary school. Mr. Pers, the teacher, who smiled showing all his gums. And mostly when he was cross.

He smiles when he is sick of us, the children whispered. But if the slightest sound reached the red-mouthed man behind his marbled desk fortification, the long cane wandered immediately out of its hiding place to harshly point out the sinner.

He pulled the girls' hair. One of them got a bald spot that started to bleed. But her father didn't dare complain. That spot won't feed lice, at any rate, Pers said.

There he comes now to pull my hair, because I'm crocheting so poorly! Ouch! No! Please let me go. I'll crochet better right away, if you let go of my hair!

"It's the hairpins, Grandmother. The hairpins. They're all tangled up, and pull your hair."

Well, help me then, lass!

The coat seamstress lived in a flat full of frieze and mothballs. They used to meet and talk about their childhood over the hand-painted coffee cups. And Tilda's son, what's become of him? And what about Irma from Backgarde?

But on a frosty day in November, there was only a hole in the ground where the house used to be. This is where the town center is going to be, the wondering coffee guest was told. Yes, but, Mrs. Gustafsson, the coat seamstress, what became of her?

The men laughed boisterously. They didn't know that, of course.

She shook her head at such indifference, and her head just kept on shaking. There were reasons enough, really. New reasons every day.

BUT UP THE HILL, there she did like going. The best view of the city. You could see a glimpse of Lake Malaren.

She sits there now and lets the sun burn the top of her thin skull. It feels like a big egg when her black summer hat's on her knees. Inside its glass wall she sees her life. It is like an Easter egg, and all the children stand neatly in the paper-green landscape. But suddenly they start swimming around. My goldfish. Poor things. To have a mother with a glass head!

Father and mother? Where are father and mother? Have to remember to ask Martha if she happens to know. Most likely not.

The sun rolls across the sky like a round and fat cheese. There he comes now and gives it a shove. He's not too proud to help. More pale than the others, he is. No sun reaches his shop. He's white as a potato sprout, and his arms are quite thin, but strong anyway.

All her girlfriends were invited to the potato-sprouting party. Toward evening, when the fragrances of springtime spread through the alleys and tickled your nose, he came with sandwiches and Swiss cheese. And if she smiled a little, and coaxed and flattered him, he even made the coffee. Women's work!

Of course. Of course I can make some coffee for you ladies! he said winking. If was fun, almost as though they were customers, the whole potato-sprouting party. And the oldest thirty-five.

She would then smooth down her shopkeeper's apron with her hands, and it was like a secret joke between them. She looked back at him pleased when he disappeared into the postage-stamp-sized yard to pump up water directly into the coffee pot. And he turned and winked with his shopkeeper's smile, and she dared smile back at him, her lips separated just a little, since now nothing could enter through them. Here she was safe, protected by women and work.

SHE MOVES UNEASILY around on the bench. Has she been sitting here talking out loud? But the young man next to her goes on with his reading and turns pages at regular intervals. Won't he ever be finished learning?

Nice to sit here in this heat after all the cellar-cool of the alleys. But she feels strangely hot and cold at the same time, until someone puts an extra blanket on her. She turns her cheek to the pillow. Have been lying here for a couple of days, it seems. Tomorrow I'll surely be well again. That is, I'm not really sick. Just a little drowsy. Going to take a look at the Old Town and see if there's been a lot of change.

She does read nicely for me, the girl.

Is that Princess Birgitta?

The window shade is blue and the sun comes through in little pinpricks. Why haven't they raised it yet? I've been awake long enough.

Carefully, slowly, she gropes for the bell. But her shoulder doesn't want to, and she sinks back. Whimpers softly like a baby chick. Will have to wait to get up then.

Was it one week ago? or two? Guess I've been sick for at least a fortnight. And so many flowers, so many flowers! So nice, people are!

"It's from your birthday, Grandmother!"

My goodness, have I had a birthday, I've forgotten all about that. I hope to God you won't get this old, lass!

"Your ninetieth birthday, Grandmother, with a birthday cake and all the telegrams that came, and we raised the flag."

Nonsense. We haven't got a flag here. Father and Mother never bought a flagpole when they couldn't afford a flag anyway. You can go ask Father.

"Grandma's father?"

Yes, who else?

But do you want me to tell you what I did yesterday?

"Well, ye...es..."

Yesterday I went up a high hill. You could see the whole town from there.

Good heavens, how small my feet have become. Am I supposed to wear such heavy stockings now, in the middle of the summer?

"Up a high hill, you said, Grandmother. Careful now. Just one more step and then sit right down in the chair. There you are! Now I'll wheel you out into the sunshine."

Up a high hill, here in Stockholm... I tell you, it was wonderfully beautiful.

I...I...I...

"Yes?"

Is that a finch singing so beautifully?

"Yes."

Can you imagine, I sat there and looked down at the town and then... Her fingers fumble across the blanket, at the newspaper. Almost tear off a piece. Traitors. Miserable, deplorable traitors!

Is this Princess Birgitta?

"Yes, it is."

Where was I now? Y. Yesterday I picked a big bunch of lilies of the valley!

Translated by EVA CLAESON

His Mother

✳   ✳   ✳   ✳   ✳

Mavis Gallant was born in Canada. She worked for a
newspaper in Montreal, but has spent most of her
adult life in Europe, and now lives in Paris. Among
her books are *The Pegnitz Junction*, *From the
Fifteenth District*, and *Home Truths*.

ℋIS MOTHER had come of age in a war and then seemed to
live a long grayness like a spun-out November. "Are you all
right?" she used to ask him at breakfast. What she really meant
was: Ask me how I am, but she was his mother and so he would
not. He leaned two fists against his temples and read a book
about photography, waiting for her to cut bread and put it on a
plate for him. He seldom looked up, never truly saw her – a
stately, careless widow with unbrushed red hair, wearing an old
fur coat over her nightgown; her last dressing gown had been
worn to ribbons and she said she had no money for another. It
seemed that nothing could stop her from telling him how she felt
or from pestering him with questions. She muttered and smoked
and drank such a lot of strong coffee that it made her bilious, and
then she would moan, "God, God, my liver! My poor head!" In
those days in Budapest you had to know the black market to find
the finest smuggled Virginia cigarettes. "Quality," she said to
him – or to his profile, rather. "Remember after I have died that
quality was important to me. I held out for the best."

She had known what it was to take excellence for granted. That was the difference between them. Out of her youth she could not recall a door slammed or a voice raised except in laughter. People had floated like golden dust; whole streets of people buoyed up by optimism, a feeling for life.

He sat reading, waiting for her to serve him. He was a stone out of a stony generation. Talking to him was like lifting a stone out of water. He never resisted, but if you let go for even a second he sank and came to rest on a dark sea floor. More than one of her soft-tempered lovers had tried to make a friend of him, but they had always given up, as they did with everything. How could she give up? She loved him. She felt ashamed because it had not been in her to control armies, history, his stony watery world. From the moment he appeared in the kitchen doorway, passive, vacant, starting to live again only because this was morning, she began all over: "Don't you feel well?" "Are you all right?" "Why can't you smile?"–though the loudest sentence was in silence: Ask me how I am.

After he left Budapest (got his first passport, flew to Glasgow with a soccer team, never came back) she became another sort of person, an émigré's mother. She shed the last of her unimportant lovers and with the money her son was soon able to send she bought a white blouse, combs that would pin her hair away from her face, and a blue kimono. She remembered long, tender conversations they had had together, and she got up early in the morning to see if a letter had come from him and then to write one of her own describing everything she thought and did. His letters to his mother said, Tell me about your headaches, are you still drinking too strong coffee, tell me the weather, the names of streets, if you still bake poppy-seed cakes.

She had never been any sort of cook, but it seemed to her that, yes, she had baked for him, perhaps in their early years together, which she looked back upon as golden, and lighter than thistledown.

On Saturday afternoons she put on a hat and soft gray gloves and went to the Vörösmarty Café. It had once had a French name, Gerbeaud, and the circle of émigrés' mothers who met to exchange news and pictures of grandchildren still called it that. "Gerbeaud" was a sign of caste and the mark of a generation, too. Like herself, the women wore hats and sometimes scarves of fur, and each carried a stuffed handbag she would not have left behind on a tabletop for even a second. Their sons' letters looked overstamped, like those he sent her now. She had not been so certain of her rank before, or felt so quietly sure, so well thought of. A social order prevailed, as it does everywhere. The aristocrats were those whose children had never left Europe; the poorest of the poor were not likely ever to see their sons again, for they had gone to Chile and South Africa. Switzerland was superior to California. A city earned more points than a town. There was no mistaking her precedence here; she was a grand duchess. If Glasgow was unfamiliar, the very sound of it somehow rang with merit. She always had a new letter to show, which was another symbol of one's station, and they were warm messages, concerned about her health, praising her remembered skill with pies and cakes. Some mothers were condemned to a lowly status only because their children forgot to write. Others had to be satisfied with notes from foreign daughters-in-law, which were often sent from table to table before an adequate reading could be obtained. Here again she was in demand, for she read three foreign languages, which suggested a background of governesses and careful schools. She might have left it at that, but her trump credentials were in plain sight. These were the gifts he bestowed – the scarves and pastel sweaters, the earrings and gloves.

What she could not do was bring the émigré ritual to its final celebration; it required a passport, a plane ticket, and a visit to the absent son. She would never deliver into his hands the three immutable presents, which were family jewelry, family photographs, and a cake. Any mother travelling to within even a few miles of another woman's son was commissioned to take all three. The cake was a bother to carry, for the traveller usually had one of her own, but who could say no? They all knew the cake's true value. Look at the way her own son claimed his share of nourishment from a mother whose cooking had always been a joke.

No one had ever been close to Scotland, and if she had not applied for her own passport or looked up flight schedules it was for a good reason: her son had never suggested she come. And yet, denied even the bliss of sewing a garnet clip into a brassiere to be smuggled to an unknown daughter-in-law, she still knew she was blessed. Other women were dismissed, forgotten. More than one had confided, "My son might as well be dead." She did not think of him as dead – how could she? – but as a coin that had dropped unheard, had rolled crazily, lay still. She knew the name of his car, of his street, she had seen pictures of them, but what did she know?

AFTER HE disappeared, as soon as she had made certain he was safe and alive, she rented his room to a student, who stayed with her for three years in conditions of some discomfort, for she had refused, at first, to remove anything belonging to her son. His books were sacred. His records were not to be played. The records had been quite valuable at one time; they were early American rock slipped in by way of Vienna and sold at a murderous rate of exchange. These collected dust now, like his albums of pictures – like the tenant student's things too, for although she pinned her hair up with combs and wore a spotless blouse, she was still no better a housekeeper. Her tenant studied forestry. He was a bumpkin, and somewhat afraid of her. She could never have mistaken him for a son. He crept in and out and brought her flowers. One day she played a record for him, to which he listened with deference rather than interest, and she remembered herself, at eighteen, hearing with the same anxious boredom a

warped scene from "Die Walküre," both singers now long dead.
Having a student in the flat did not make her feel she was in
touch with her son, or even with his generation. His room
changed meanwhile; even its smell was no longer the same. She
began to wonder what his voice had been like. She could see him,
she dreamed of him often, but her dreams and memories were
like films with the sound track removed.

The bumpkin departed, and she took in his place a future art
historian – the regime produced these in awesome numbers
now – who gave way, in turn, to the neurasthenic widow of a
poet. The poet's widow was taken over in time by her children,
and replaced by a couple of young librarians. And then came two
persons not quite chosen by herself. She could have refused
them, but thought it wiser not to. They were an old man and his
pregnant granddaughter. They seemed to be brokenly poor; the
granddaughter almost to the end of her term worked long hours
in a plasma laboratory. And yet they appeared endowed with
dark, important connections: no sooner were they installed than
she was granted a telephone, which her tenants never used without asking, and only for laconic messages – the grandfather to
state that his granddaughter was not yet at home, or the girl to
take down the day and hour of a meeting somewhere. After the
granddaughter had her baby they became four in a flat that had
barely been comfortable for two. She cleared out the last of her
son's records and his remaining books (the rest had long ago
been sold or stolen), and she tried to establish a set of rules. For
one, she made it a point to remain in the kitchen when her tenants took their meals. This was her home; it was not strictly a
shared and still less a communal Russian apartment. But she
could go only so far: it was at Gerbeaud's that she ranked as a
grand duchess. These people reckoned differently, and on their
terms she was, if not at the foot of the ladder, then dangerously
to one side of it; she had an émigré son, she received gifts and
money from abroad, and she led in terms of the common good a

parasitic existence. They were careful, even polite, but they were installed. She was inhabited by them, as by an illness one must learn to endure.

It was around this time – when her careless, undusted, but somehow pure rooms became a slum, festooned with washing, reeking of boiling milk, where she was seldom alone or quiet – that she began to drift away from an idea she had held about her age and time. Where, exactly, was the youth she recalled as happy? What had been its shape, its color? All that golden dust had not belonged to her – it had been part of her mother. It was her mother who had floated like thistledown, smiled, lived with three servants on call, stood with a false charming gaucherie, an arm behind her, an elbow grasped. That simulated awkwardness took suppleness and training; it required something her generation had not been granted, which was time. Her mother had let her coat fall on the floor because coats were replaceable then, not only because there had been someone to pick it up. She had carried a little curling iron in her handbag. When she quarrelled with her husband, she went to the station and climbed into a train marked "Budapest-Vienna-Rome," and her husband had thought it no more than amusing to have to fetch her back. Slowly, as "eighteen" came to mean an age much younger than her son's, as he grew older in Scotland, married, had a child, began slipping English words into his letters, went on about fictitious apple or poppy-seed cakes, she parted without pain from a soft, troubled memory, from an old gray film about porters wheeling steamer trunks, white fur wraps, bunches of violets, champagne. It was gone: it had never been. She and her son were both mistaken, and yet they had never been closer. Now that she had the telephone, he called her on Easter Sunday, and on Christmas Eve, and on her birthday. His wife had spoken to her in English:

"It's snowing here. Is it snowing in Budapest?"

"It quite often snows."

"I hope we can meet soon."

"That would be pleasant."

His wife's parents sent her Christmas greetings with stern Biblical messages, as if they judged her, by way of her son, to be frivolous, without a proper God. At least they knew now that she spoke correct English; on the other hand, perhaps they were simple souls unable to imagine that anything but English could ever be.

They were not out of touch; nor did he neglect her. No one could say that he had. He had never missed a monthly transfer of money, he was faithful about sending his overstamped letters and the colored snapshots of his wife, his child, their Christmas tree, and his wife's parents side by side upon a modern-looking sofa. One unposed picture had him up a ladder pasting sheets of plastic tiles on a kitchen wall. She could not understand the meaning of this photograph, in which he wore jeans and a sweater that might have been knitted by an untalented child. His hair had grown long, it straggled in brown mouse-tails over the collar of the lamentable pullover. He stood in profile, so that she could see just half of a new and abundant mustache. Also – and this might have been owing to the way he stood, because he had to sway to hold his balance – he looked as if he might have become, well, a trifle stout. This was a picture she never showed anyone at Vörösmarty Place, though she examined it often, by several kinds of light. What did it mean, what was its secret expression? She looked for the invisible ink that might describe her son as a husband and father. He was twenty-eight, he had a mustache, he worked in his own home as a common laborer.

She said to herself, I never let him lift a finger. I waited on him from the time he opened his eyes.

In response to the ladder picture she employed a photographer, a former schoolfriend of her son's, to take a fiercely lighted portrait of her sitting on her divan-bed with a volume of Impressionist reproductions opened on her lap. She wore a string of garnets and turned her head proudly, without gaping or grinning. From the background wall she had removed a picture of clouds taken by her son, then a talented amateur, and hung in its stead a framed parchment that proved her mother's family had been ennobled. Actually a whole town had been ennobled at a stroke, but the parchment was legal and real. Normally it would not have been in her to display the skin of the dog, as these things were named, but perhaps her son's wife, looking at the new proud picture of his mother, might inquire, "What is that, there on the wall?"

She wrote him almost every morning – she had for years, now. At night her thoughts were morbid, unchecked, and she might have been likely to tell about her dreams or to describe the insignificant sadness of a lifetime, or to recall the mornings when he had eaten breakfast in silence, when talking to him had been like lifting a stone. Her letters held none of those things. She wrote wearing her blue, clean, now elderly kimono, sitting at the end of her kitchen table, while her tenants ate and quarrelled endlessly.

She had a long back-slanting hand she had once been told was the hand of a liar. Upside down the letter looked like a shower of rain. It was strange, mysterious, she wrote, to be here in the kitchen with the winter sun on the sparkling window (it was grimy, in fact; but she was seeing quite another window as she wrote) and the tenant granddaughter, whose name was Ilona, home late on a weekday. Ilona and the baby and the grandfather were all three going to a funeral this morning. It seemd a joyous sort of excursion because someone was fetching them by car; that in itself was an indication of their sombre connections. It explained, in shorthand, why she had not squarely refused to take them in. She wrote that the neighbors' radios could be heard faintly like the sounds of life breaking into a fever, and about Ilona preparing a boiled egg for the baby, drawing a face on the shell to make it interesting, and the baby opening his mouth, patting the table in a broken rhythm, patting crumbs with a spreadout hand. Here in the old kitchen she shared a wintry, secret, morning life with strangers.

Grandfather wore a hearing aid, but he had taken it apart, and it lay now on the table like parts of a doll's skull. Wearing it at breakfast kept him from enjoying his food. Spectacles bothered him, too. He made a noise eating, because he could not hear himself; nor did he see the mess around his cup and plate.

"Worse than an infant!" his granddaughter cried. She had a cross-looking little Tartar face. She tore squares of newspaper, one to go on the floor, another for underneath his plate. He scattered sugar and pipe ash and crusts and the pieces of his hearing aid. At the same time he was trying to attend to a crossword puzzle, which he looked at with a magnifying glass. But he still would not put his spectacles on, because they interfered with his food. Being deaf, he travelled alone in his memories and sometimes came out with just anything. His mind plodded back and forth. Looking up from the puzzle he said loudly, "My granddaughter has a diploma. Indeed she has. She worked in a hospital. Yes, she did. Some people think too much of themselves when they have a diploma. They begin to speak pure Hungarian. They try to speak like educated people. Not Ilona! You will never hear one word of good Hungarian from *her*!"

His granddaughter had just untied a towel she used as a bib for the child. She grimaced and buried her Tartar's grimace in the towel. Only her brown hair was seen, and her shaking shoulders. She might have been laughing. Her grandfather wore a benign and rather a foolish smile until she looked up and screamed, "I hate you." She reminded him of all that she had done to make him happy. She described the last place they'd lived in, the water gurgling in the pipes, the smell of bedbugs. She had found this splendid apartment; she was paying their rent. His little pension scarcely covered the coffee he drank. "You thought your son was too good for my mother," she said. "You made her miserable, too."

The old man could not hear any of this. His shaking freckled hands had been assembling the hearing aid. He adjusted it in time to hear Ilona say, "It is hard to be given lessons in correct speech by someone who eats like a pig."

He sighed and said only, "Children," as one might sound resigned to any natural enemy.

The émigré's mother, their landlady, had stopped writing. She looked up, not at them, but of course they believed they could be seen. They began to talk about their past family history, as they did when they became tense and excited, and it all went into the letter. Ilona had lost her father, her mother, and her little sister in a road accident when, with Grandfather, they had been on their way to a funeral in the suburbs in a bus.

Funerals seemed to be the only outing they ever enjoyed. The old man listened to Ilona telling it again, but presently he got up and left them, as if the death of his son allowed him no relief even so many years later. When he came back he had his hat and coat on. For some reason, he had misunderstood and thought they had to leave at once for the new excursion. He took his landlady's hand and pumped it up and down, saying, "From the bottom of my heart . . . ," though all he was leading up to was "Goodbye." He did not let her hand go until he inadvertently brought it down hard on a thick cup.

"He has always embarrassed us in public," said Ilona, clearing away. "What could we do? He was my father's father."

That other time, said the old man – calmed now, sitting down in his overcoat – the day of the *fatal* funeral, there had been time to spare, out in a suburb, where they had to change from one bus to another. They had walked once around a frozen duckpond. He had been amazed, the old man remembered, at how many people were free on a working weekday. His son carried one of the children; little Ilona walked.

"Of course I walked! I was twelve!" she screamed from the sink.

He had been afraid that Ilona would never learn to speak, because her mother said everything for her. When Ilona pointed
with her woolly fist, her mother crooned, "Skaters." Or else she
announced, "You are cold," and pulled a scarf up over Ilona's
apple cheeks.

"That was my sister," Ilona said. "I was twelve."

"Now, a governess might have made the child speak, say
words correctly," said the old man. "Mothers are helpless. They
can only say yes, yes, and try to repeat what the child seems to be
thinking."

"He has always embarrassed us," Ilona said. "My mother
hated going anywhere in his company."

Once around the duckpond, and then an old bus rattled up
and they got in. The driver was late, and to make up for time he
drove fast. At the bottom of a hill, on a wide sheet of black ice,
the bus turned like a balky horse, rocked, steadied, and the
driver threw himself over the wheel as if to protect it. An army
lorry came down the hill, the first of two. Ilona's mother pulled
the baby against her and pulled Ilona's head on her lap.

"Eight killed, including the two drivers," Ilona said.

Here was their folklore, their richness; how many persons
have lost their families on a bus and survived to describe the ho-
locaust? No wonder she and Grandfather were still together. If
she had not married her child's father, it was because he had not
wanted Grandfather to live with them. "You, yes," he had said
to Ilona. "Relatives, no." Grandfather nodded, for he was used
to hearing this. Her cold sacrifice always came on top of his dis-
approval.

Well, that was not quite the truth of it, the émigré's mother
went on writing. The man who had interceded for them, whom
she had felt it was wiser not to refuse, who might be the child's
father, had been married for quite a long time.

The old man looked blank and strained. His eyes had become
small. He looked Chinese. "Where we lived then was a good

place to live with children," he said, perhaps speaking of a quarter fading like the edge of a watercolor into gray apartment blocks. Something had frightened him. He took out a clean pocket handkerchief and held it to his lips.

"Another army lorry took us to the hospital," said Ilona, "Do you know what you were saying?"

He remembered an ambulance. He and his grandchild had been wrapped in blankets, had lain on two stretchers, side by side, fingers locked together. That was what he remembered.

"You said, *'My mother, my mother'*," she told him.

"I don't think I said that."

Now they are having their usual disagreement, she wrote her son. Lorry or ambulance?

"I heard," said Ilona. "I was conscious."

"I had no reason. If I said, 'My mother,' I was thinking, 'My children'."

The rainstorm would cover pages more. Her letter had veered off and resembled her thoughts at night. She began to tell him she had trouble sleeping. She had been given a wonderful new drug, but unfortunately it was habit-forming and the doctor would not renew it. The drug gave her a deep sleep, from which she emerged fresh and enlivened, as if she had been swimming. During the sleep she was allowed exact and colored dreams in which she was a young girl again and men long dead came to visit. They sat amiably discussing their deaths. Her first fiancé, killed in 1943, opened his shirt to show the chest wound. He apologized for having died without warning. He did not know that less than a year later she had married another man. The dead had no knowledge of love beyond the span of their own lives. The next night, she found herself with her son's father. They were standing together buying tickets for a play when she realized he was dead. He stood in his postwar shabbiness, discreet, hidden mind, camouflàged face, and he had ceased to be with the living. Her grief was so cruel that, lest she perish in sleep from the shock of it, someone unseen but conciliating suggested that she trade any person she knew in order to keep him with her. He would never have the misery of knowing that he was dead.

What would her son say to all this? My mother is now at an age when women dream of dead men, he might tell himself; when they begin to choose quite carelessly between the dead and the living. Women are crafty even in their sleep. They know they will survive. Why weep? Why discuss? Why let things annoy you? For a long time she believed he had left because he could not look at her life. Perhaps his going had been as artless, as simple, as he still insisted: he had got his first passport, flown out with a football team, never come back. He was between the dead and the living, a voice on the telephone, an affectionate letter full of English words, a coin rolled and lying somewhere in secret. And she, she was the revered and respected mother of a generous, an attentive, a camouflaged stranger.

Tell me the weather, he still wrote. Tell me the names of streets. She began a new page: Vörösmarty Place, if you remember, is at the beginning of Váci Street, the oldest street in the Old City. In the middle of the Place stands a little park. Our great poet, for whom the Place is named, sits carved in marble. Sculptured figures look gratefully up to him. They are grateful because he is the author of the national anthem. There are plane trees full of sparrows, and there are bus stops, and even a little Métro, the oldest in Europe, perhaps old-fashioned, but practical – it goes to the Zoo, the Fine Arts Museum, the Museum of Decorative Art, the Academy of Music, and the Opera. The old redoubt is there, too, at least one wall of it, backed up to a new building where you go to book seats for concerts. The real face of the redoubt has been in ruins since the end of the war. It used to be Moorish-romantic. The old part, which gave on the Danube, had in her day – no, in her mother's day – been a large concert hall, the reconstruction of which created grave problems because of modern acoustics. At Gerbeaud's the pastries are still the best in Europe, she wrote, and so are the prices. There are five or six little rooms, little marble tables, comfortable chairs. Between the stiff lace curtains and the windowpanes are quite valuable pieces of china. In summer one can sit on the pavement. There is enough space between the plane trees, and the ladies with their elegant hats are not in too much danger from the sparrows. If you come there, you will see younger people, too, and foreigners, and women who wait for foreigners, but most of the customers, yes, most, belong to the magic circle of mothers whose children have gone away. The café opens at ten and closes at nine. It is always crowded. "You can often find me there," she went on, "and without fail every Saturday," as if she might look up and see him draw near, transformed, amnesiac, not knowing her. I hope that I am not in your dreams, she said, because dreams are populated by the silent and the dead, and I still speak, I am alive. I wear a hat with a brim and soft gray gloves. I read their letters in three foreign languages. Thanks to you, I can order an endless succession of little cakes, I can even sip cognac. Will you still know me? I was your mother.

The Electric Typewriter

*   *   *   *   *

Francesca Sanvitale was born in Milan, studied and
worked in Florence until the 1960s, and then moved
to Rome where she still lives. She has published
three novels and many essays on contemporary
fiction.

*T*HE RAINY SEPTEMBER cast a low, melancholy, beautiful
light. Day after day it caused feelings of detachment and separation, even despair, especially at sunset.

For hours Carlo hadn't moved and had passed the idle afternoon without enjoying the September light. His gaze had shifted
from the bookshelves, and slowly moved from one object to another. Like one wretched, depraved, or obsessed, he had stared
at the orderly piles of newspapers and magazines on little
benches and tables, separated according to a personal work
method, and gazed at the flowers in the rugs, the elaborately dec-
orated borders. Everything scrutinized in detail but without
thought.

He had been trying to pursue, gather, differentiate, and
thereby destroy a fog behind his eyes that came out to cloud his
glasses. This fog had a peculiar characteristic: it dissolved back-
grounds and perspectives and outlined things in dusty lights.

For more than a month he had calmed his aggravating restlessness by devoting the entire afternoon to the observation of his studio and he no longer felt the need to go out.

Iris would come back soon and he was waiting for her. His eyes stopped searching the shadows and were cast outside himself, like an object in a surrealistic painting, towards an imagined door. Everything would return to normal in his sight and in the room as soon as Iris turned the key in the lock. As always she would slam the door carelessly and break into his space. She would open a window and lean out, exposing her fat hips, crying out, "Air! Air!" She would observe with disgust the ashtray full of butts. She would hurriedly question him ("How many pages?" "Have you finished?" How far did you get?").

Out of habit Carlo would not answer. From the kitchen would come the smells of garlic and onion that he found reassuring. The workday was over. In other times, which seemed far away but were not, they would see friends in the evening, go to the theater or a movie.

He had turned sixty-two the day before. Many said he was a great writer, but not too prolific. He had noticed that after sixty almost all writers, for one reason or another, become great writers. The public is lavish with its praise and then forgets all about them.

He gazed at the books, the objects of various size and value, pictures, rugs, armchairs, divans, and observed that this was what remained of the many words used which formed neither emotions nor memories. They had materialized there around him as if he had been the manager of a small, agoraphobic business for forty years.

For him and Iris almost forty years of artistic activity had transformed themselves into a series of objects contained in that middle-class apartment and in the small seaside apartment. His stories were born one after the other with relative ease, and he was convinced that they were always significant. Iris had said repeatedly in the face of his uncertainties and anxieties: just write and don't think about it too much. It's all right, it's all right. You are an artist.

And the future? the future? This had been the past: an introduction, indeed a necessary introduction. He was sure that the future would be different in the sense that he finally would grasp something that he had only vaguely sought inside himself, he would plunge into the surging depths that exist below human surfaces. Maybe he would sell the two apartments. Maybe he would move abroad. Maybe Iris would die.

Iris kept saying with love or with scorn or with a particular maternal inflection that he was an eternal child. This was the way she forced him in bed to touch the depths of his weakness, and at the moment he understood it she would brush it away with a sleight-of-hand. In a kind of dream, a show *ad absurdum*, he found himself practicing a virility without tenderness, only frenzy, and in that kind of game or dream he was the tyrant and she the slave.

Iris was very fat and had become old. She didn't care. She seemed to believe that their nights would never change. She had assumed the role of trainer and in the morning Carlo was ready for the ring of his studio, at the desk, strictly tied to her and to that room, unfit for life or any other kind of woman. He still desired Iris because she allowed him the vices his mind needed. Iris barred any novelty, she obliterated defeats. She prevented a calm reflection on the meaning of existence, but she also prevented thought from sinking into darkness, beyond the curtain of flowing images.

For a month his depression had deepened and his headaches, anxiety, and tiredness had increased. He was forced to withdraw into himself. The doctor and Iris consulted behind his back. He had come to a passage, perhaps providential: he had to reflect, to understand something that had escaped him. Then he could go on.

He was not writing anymore. That didn't matter. He was too

tired, trapped in a dismal listlessness. His face played annoying
tricks, but the doctor said the symptoms were entirely gratuitous
and connected with his nerves. The same with the nausea that
every once in a while rose from his guts for no reason. He had to
let himself rest.

He went out on the balcony and looked to the left toward the
neighboring balcony. Almost dark. The other window was illuminated. He heard the regular, muffled noise of the electric
typewriter. Short pauses, followed by a clicking. He sat down,
even though the cool wind bothered him. He watched the wind
shaking the stems of the long, thin, nearly wilted carnations that
Orlando, the next-door neighbor, didn't take care of. They
drooped over the railing in small dry clusters.

He was aware of the traffic on the street. He listened to the
stopping and starting of the electric typewriter. With an idiotic
joy every day he tried to imagine what in the world Orlando was
writing. It might be a new novel. He had already written two of
them, very much like two stories, and not much longer. Compe-
tent representations. Pleasant female characters. Plausible dialogue. The stories that Orlando told were easy to understand.
Orlando himself was more difficult to understand.

Since he had to rest, Carlo often amused himself by inventing
stories to the rhythm of the electric typewriter. He was free to
tell himself nonsensical stories, imitating the avant-garde buried
before his youth. He drew out and put together odd bunches of
images in the surrealistic manner, or composed obscene love
songs, or sonnets in the manner of Carducci. It was his solitary
and entirely new way to play in the dark silence and also to feel
that his mind, like an enclosed reservoir, was full of words that
mingled in amazing fantasies even without his willing them. He
seemed to have regained a sense of freedom, a taste of childhood,
of adolescence.

From Orlando's apartment came a longer caesura than usual.
Immediately Carlo imagined in the darkness before him the gi-

gantic ectoplasm of a hand suspended over the keyboard and he waited. He thought only one exact phrase: maybe that clicking will never start up again.

In that case, in such an extraordinary and unprecedented case, the silence would become high, magnificent, charged with emotion. Orlando and he, like two astronauts detached from their spaceship would move away into empty space grasping each other tightly, quickly disappearing, exactly alike and mute. But the clicking recommenced and Carlo heard within it the arrogant superiority of youth.

Orlando lived alone. He wrote articles for a newspaper and was a researcher at the university. A girl named Gina visited him at irregular intervals and lived with him for two or three days. Carlo had never understood their real relationship. One could suppose it a stability that had lasted for years. Or a complete casualness that had kept them apart as it had united them. He spied on them. They kept a rhythmical pace on the street as they walked in step. They dressed alike, faded jeans and nice sweaters, colored shirts, jackets. They gave the impression of cautious confidence and harmony. They had the habit of stopping every once in a while as they walked and looking into each other's eyes with a slight smile. Gina would toss back her long straight hair with a loose, careless motion, and bending her head would gather it in one hand, bringing it forward over her shoulders.

Carlo watched them as if they were two people to be robbed. Their affectations as a couple, their over-harmonious movements made him feel spiteful. He criticized them: according to him they were showing off on a stage and Orlando would have to watch out because that was not life.

In a certain sense he desired both of them. He allowed himself sexual fantasies or extravagant erotic impulses because he knew he was depressed and wanted to amuse himself. Orlando was thirty, slender as a fifteen-year-old but without the aggressiveness. He went through the world taking his pleasures with a casual elegance and a secret obstinacy. Carlo envied him with an intensity and confusion so strong that at times it seemed like love.

The doorbell rang. Carlo shuffled down the hall and opened the door.

"Excuse me for bothering you. Can you lend me your Collins?"

Orlando spoke with a pleasant urbanity.

Carlo made a brusque gesture, turned on the lights, preceded him into the studio. Orlando's self-assurance was stupid. Why on earth did he have to have that particular dictionary? He bent over with difficulty and his head spun. A whirl, a dangerous dizziness, passed through his brain.

"Here is the Collins," he said, panting a little. "I have it by chance." He was observing Orlando's body: his well-built arms with long muscles, his chest and slender hips. He possessed a supple gracefulness, a suggestion of boyishness with his sudden gestures. His eyes were slightly convex, clear and very still, like those of certain insects.

Orlando looked around, a little unsure of himself. "I see," he remarked, in a tone of respect by no means humble, "that you have the Tommaseo Bellini dictionary in the first edition of eight volumes!" He made a slight gesture toward the volumes.

Carlo said nothing. There was a pause. Orlando began to say that he would be leaving for New York the next day. "On a scholarship for one year. I wanted to say good-bye because I'm leaving my apartment. I'm sorry I didn't see more of you." He stopped. He frowned and added, "Naturally it was unavoidable. It's hard for anyone who writes in the province...."

Carlo gave him an uncomprehending look and interrupted him: "The province? What has the province to do with it?"

"I meant Italy. The games they play everywhere...."

He smiled.

Silence reigned. Carlo straightened some newspapers. "One

can write anywhere," he mumbled. He was about to add something else but Orlando was heading rapidly toward the front
door. "I'll bring it back right away," he said in a high voice.
Shrill, a sort of warble.

Carlo was alone again. He turned off the lights. Over
Orlando's bed was an Escher poster. In the living room a few
pieces of light wood furniture, red and black director's chairs.
Basically the boy was almost poor and, compared to him, lived
like an ascetic. He didn't own a house and earned little. He
owned only an electric typewriter. But Orlando made him angry: he didn't realize the complexity of the problem, he didn't
even understand that he was dealing more with an enigma than a
profession. Or both? At this point he became angry with himself
also. That happened to someone suffering from nerves: small
exterior events, little upsets resulted in inner disturbances. Orlando was going to New York and consequently Carlo wouldn't
be able to know what turn that life had taken. This bothered
him, annoyed him very much. In six months of being close
neighbors they had talked only foolishness, letting the two
women take the lead in their rare encounters. Did he like Con-
rad? Did he like James? Had he read, for instance, *Kiss of the
Spider Woman*? What was the plot of the novel he was writing?
and *his* novels? what did he *really* think of them?

He didn't hear the clicking any more. A particular silence fell
over the house and over him.

The lock turned and in a moment Iris was in the studio.

"Well," she said at once. Her voice left no doubt of her inva-
sion. "Still in the dark?" She turned on the light and began taking in everything with her inspection. "Nasty weather outside. It
seems like winter. Better to stay in the house." She threw a newspaper on the desk. "The interview came out. The photograph of
you doesn't look bad. If I were a young reader it would give me
wicked thoughts." She giggled. She took the ashtray.

"What is there to eat?" Carlo asked.

"Nothing, why?" She broke into one of her typical laughs. It would be a special dish, then. She went into the hall exclaiming, "I can't wait to take off my shoes!"

For a moment he thought of following her, of taking her by the shoulders, of making love quickly, before supper, as they used to do when they were young. He sat down and lowered his head in his hands. Again the doorbell as he tried to rouse himself from his torpor. Orlando was already back with the dictionary and was looking at him quizzically. "Aren't you feeling well?" He stepped forward to hold him up or give him support, but Carlo shook his head, overcome by anger and drowsiness. "Certainly not," he managed to say in a kind of whisper. "Nothing is wrong, nothing, do you understand?"

Orlando moved back to reestablish the space he had violated.

"Just remember!" Carlo believed he was shouting, "Just remember that you don't kid around with words!" But he only thought he was shouting and he had lost the thought again. That wasn't what he wanted to throw in Orlando's face to waken him from his conventional faith.

The only words that came to his mind were even more senseless: have you read Tolstoy? Have you read Stendhal? and Dickens? and De Quincey? and Dickinson? and Chekhov? and Goethe? and Dostoevski? and . . .

He was forming a kind of litany in his head that numbed him as though he were counting sheep to go to sleep. He closed his eyes.

Orlando stood there stock-still, in amazement, looking at him. He barely murmured, "I wanted to say good-bye, excuse me." Nothing happened. Carlo's heavy body folded over in a slow-motion faint and his eyelids opened and closed as if he had swallowed poison. His eyes were rolling wildly.

Orlando backed away in little steps. "Signora Iris," he murmured again. "I don't think Signor Carlo feels very well."

Iris came out unconcerned and shook her head. "It's nerves, depression," she said.

"I'm so sorry," whispered Orlando. "I'm sure he'll feel better soon. Please give him my best wishes."

Carlo heard Iris and Orlando talking and saying good-bye. He heard him go out. He heard the noises that punctuated his afternoons: the turn of the lock, the click of light. He felt that he was sinking into a deep hell: perhaps it was really the well he had dreamed up, the darkness that leads to consciousness, to the horror that right words come from. He had avoided it all his life and he wasn't sure he wanted this ordeal. "Iris," he shouted, "Iris! Iris!"

A menacing silence fell. The shadow assailed him, forced pain on him. What was this empty room of knowledge that, like a twin to torture, his nightmare symbolized? He thought confusedly of Orpheus, of Pamino, of efforts, of hard labors described in fables, and was about to grasp the meaning of what he was seeking, as if it were something struggling to enter his heart with simple clarity. Perhaps they were the true words, the unforgettable stories. "Iris!" he shouted again. He stood up staggering, nerve-racked and shaken by so much emotion. Suddenly he vomited.

The doorbell rang for the third time. Iris ran to the door and opened it.

"How is he today?" the doctor said as he entered.

Iris dried a tear with the palm of her hand. "He seems worse to me." She spoke softly to keep Carlo from hearing. "Much worse. But he doesn't realize...he has never realized anything...."

The doctor clapped her on the back. "Cheer up, Signora," he said good-naturedly. "Let's go and have a look at him."

Translated by M A R T H A K I N G

Okkervil River

* * * * *

Tatyana Tolstaya was born in Leningrad in 1951, and now lives in Moscow. Her stories appear frequently in Soviet journals, and in the *New Yorker*. Her story collection is titled *On the Golden Porch*.

*W*HEN THE SUN moved into the sign of Scorpio, it grew very windy, dark, and rainy. The wet, streaming city, banging wind against the glass outside the defenseless, uncurtained, bachelor's window with processed cheeses cooling between the panes on the sill, seemed to be Peter's evil plan, the revenge of the huge, bug-eyed, big-mouthed and toothy carpenter-tsar, ship's axe in his upraised hand, chasing and gaining on his weak and terrified subjects in their nightmares. The rivers, rushing out to the windblown and threatening sea, bucked and with hissing urgency opened the cast-iron hatches and quickly raised their watery backs in museum cellars, licking at the fragile collections that were crumbling into damp sand, at shamans' masks made of rooster feathers, at crooked foreign swords, at beaded robes, and at the sinewy feet of the angry museum staff brought from their beds in the middle of the night. On days like that, when the rain, darkness, and window-bending wind reflected the white solemn face of loneliness, Simeonov, feeling particularly big-nosed and balding and particularly feeling his years around his face and his cheap socks far below, on the edge of existence, would put on the teakettle, wipe dust with his sleeve from the table, clearing away the books that stuck out their white bookmark tongues, set up the gramophone, selecting the right-sized book to support its listing side, and in blissful anticipation pull out Vera Vasilevna from the torn and yellow-stained jacket – an old and heavy disc, anthracite in color, and not disfigured by smooth concentric circles – one love song on each side.

"No! it's not you! I love! so passionately!" Vera Vasilevna skipped, creaking and hissing, quickly spinning under the needle; the hiss creak and spin formed a black tunnel that widened into the gramophone horn, and triumphant in her victory over Simeonov, speeding out of the festooned orchid of her voice, divine, low, dark, lacy and dusty at first and then throbbing with underwater pressure, rising up from the depths, transforming, trembling on the water like flames –*pshsts-pshsts-pshsts, pshsts-pshsts-pshsts* – filling like a sail, getting louder, breaking hawsers, speeding unrestrained *pshsts-pshsts-pshsts* a caravel over the nocturnal waters splashing flames – stronger – spreading its wings, gathering speed, smoothly tearing away from the remaining bulk of the flow that had given birth to it, away from the tiny Simeonov left on shore, his balding bare head lifted to the gigantic, glowing, dimming half sky to the voice coming in a triumphant cry – no, it wasn't he whom Vera Vasilevna loved so passionately, but still, essentially, she loved only him, and it was mutual. *Kh-shch-shch-shch.*

Simeonov carefully removed the now silent Vera Vasilevna, shaking the record, holding it between straightened, respectful hands; he examined the ancient label: Ah, where are you now, Vera Vasilevna? Where are your white bones now? And turning her over on her back, he placed the needle, squinting at the olive-black shimmer of the bobbing thick disc, and listened once more, longing for the long-faded, *pshsts*, chrysanthemums in the garden, *pshsts*, where they had met, and once again, gathering underwater pressure, throwing off dust, laces, and years, Vera Vasilevna creaked and appeared as a languorous naiad – an unathletic, slightly plump turn-of-the-century naiad – O sweet pear, guitar, hourglass, slope-hipped champagne bottle!

And by then the teakettle would be aboil, and Simeonov, fishing some processed cheese or ham scraps from the windowsill, would put the record on again and have a bachelor feast off a newspaper, delighting in the fact that Tamara would not find him today, would not disturb his precious rendezvous with Vera Vasilevna. He was happy alone in his small apartment, alone with Vera Vasilevna. The door was securely locked against Tamara, and the tea was strong and sweet, and the translation of the unneeded book from the rare language was almost complete – he would have money soon, and Simeonov would buy a scarce record from a shark for a high price, one where Vera Vasilevna regrets that spring will come but not for her – a man's romance, a romance of solitude, and the incorporeal Vera Vasilevna will sing it, merging with Simeonov into a single longing, sobbing voice. O blessed solitude! Solitude eats right out of the frying pan, spears a cold meat patty from a murky half-liter jar, makes tea right in the mug – so what? Peace and freedom! A family rattles the dish cupboard, sets out traps of cups and saucers, catches your soul with knife and fork – gets it under the ribs from both sides – smothers it with a tea caddy, tosses a tablecloth over its head, but the free lone soul slips out through the linen fringe, squeezes like an eel through the napkin ring and – *hop! catch me if you can!* – it's back in the dark magical circle filled with flames, outlined by Vera Vasilevna's voice, following her skirts and fan from the bright ballroom out onto the summer balcony at night, the spacious semicircle above a sweet-smelling bed of chrysanthemums; well, actually, their white, dry, and bitter aroma is an autumnal one, a harbinger of fall separation, oblivion, but love still lives in my ailing heart – a sickly smell, the smell of sadness and decay, *where are you now, Vera Vasilevna,* perhaps in Paris or Shanghai and which rain – Parisian light blue or Chinese yellow – drizzles over your grave, and whose soil chills your white bones? *No, it's not you I love so passionately.* (That's what you say. Of course it's me, Vera Vasilevna.)

Trolleys passed Simeonov's window, once upon a time clanging their bells and swinging the hanging loops that resembled stirrups – Simeonov kept thinking that the horses were hidden up in the ceiling, like portraits of trolley ancestors taken up to the attic; but the bells grew still, and now all he heard was the rattle, clickety-clack and squeals on the turns, and at last the red-sided cars with wooden benches died, and the new cars were rounded, noiseless, hissing at stops, and you could sit, plopping down on the soft seat that gasped and gave up the ghost beneath you, and ride off into the blue yonder to the last stop, beckoning with its name: *Okkervil River.* But Simeonov had never gone there. It was the end of the world and there was nothing there for him, but that wasn't it, really: without seeing or knowing that distant, almost non-Leningrad river, he could imagine it in any way he chose: a murky greenish flow, for instance, with a slow green sun murkily floating in it, silvery willows softly hanging down from the gentle bank, red brick two-story houses with tile roofs, humped wooden bridges – a quiet world in a sleepy stupor; but actually it was probably filled with warehouses, fences, and some stinking factory spitting out mother-of-pearl toxic gases, a dump smoldering smelly smoke, or something else hopeless, provincial, and trite. No, no reason to be disillusioned by going to Okkervil River, it was better to mentally plant long-haired willows on its banks, set up steep-roofed houses, release slow-moving residents, perhaps in German caps, striped stockings, with long porcelain pipes in their mouths. . . even better to pave the Okkervil's embankment, fill the river with gray water, sketch in bridges with towers and chains, smooth out the granite parapets with a curved template, line the embankment with tall gray houses with cast-iron grates on the windows – with a fish-scale motif on top of the gates and nasturtiums peeking from the balconies—and settle young Vera Vasilevna there and let her walk, pulling on a long glove, along the paving stones, placing her feet close together, stepping daintily with her black snub-toed slippers with apple-round heels, in a small round hat with a veil, through the still drizzle of a St. Petersburg morning; and in that case, make the fog light blue.

Let's have light blue fog. The fog in place, Vera Vasilevna walks, her round heels clicking, across the entire paved section held in Simeonov's imagination, here's the edge of the scenery, the director's run out of means, he is powerless and weary, he releases the actors, crosses out the balconies with nasturtiums, gives those who like it the grating with fish-scale motif, flicks the granite parapets into the water, stuffs the towered bridges into his pockets—the pockets bulge, the chains droop as if from grandfather's watch, and only the Okkervil River flows on, narrowing and widening feverishly, unable to select a permanent image for itself.

Simeonov ate processed cheese, translated boring books, sometimes brought women home in the evenings and in the morning, disappointed, saw them out—*no! it's not you!*—hid from Tamara, who kept coming over with washed laundry and fried potatoes and flowered curtains for the windows, and who assiduously kept forgetting the important things at Simeonov's—hairpins or a handkerchief she needed urgently by nightfall, and she would travel across the whole city to get them, and Simeonov would put out the light and stand pressed against the foyer wall while she banged on the door, and very often he gave in, and then he had a hot meal for dinner and drank strong tea from a blue and gold cup and had homemade cookies for dessert, and it was too late for Tamara to go back home, of course; the last trolley had gone and it wouldn't reach the foggy Okkervil River, and Tamara would fluff up the pillows while Vera Vasilevna—turning her back and not listening to Simeonov's explanations – would walk into the night along the embankment, swaying on her apple-round heels.

The autumn was thickening when he purchased a heavy disc, chipped on one side, from a shark – they had haggled over the damage, the price was very high, and why? because Vera Vasilevna was forgotten, was never played on the radio, never flashed in a newsreel, and now only refined eccentrics, snobs, amateurs, and aesthetes who felt like throwing money on the incorporeal chased after her records, collected wire recordings, transcribed her low, dark voice that glowed like aged wine. *The old woman's still alive*, the shark said, she lives somewhere in Leningrad, in poverty, they say, and shabbiness, she didn't shine too long in her day, either; she lost her diamonds, husband, apartment, son, two lovers, and finally her voice: in that order; and she managed to handle all those losses before she was thirty-five, and she stopped singing back then, though she's still alive. So that's how it is, thought Simeonov with heavy heart on the way home over bridges and through gardens, across trolley tracks, thinking *that's how it is . . . .* And locking the door, making tea, he put on his newly acquired treasure and, looking out the window at the heavy colored clouds looming on the sunset side, he built, as usual, a section of the granite embankment, and erected a bridge: the towers were heavier this time, and the chains were very cast iron, and the wind ruffled and wrinkled, agitated the broad gray smoothness of the Okkervil River, and Vera Vasilevna, tripping more than she ought in her uncomfortable heels invented by Simeonov, wrung her hands and bent her neatly coiffed head toward her sloping little shoulder – the moon glowed so softly, so softly, and my thoughts are full of you – the moon wouldn't cooperate and slipped out like soap from his hands, sliding across the Okkervil clouds – there were always problems with the Okkervil skies – how restlessly the transparent, tamed shadows of our imagination scurry when the noises and smells of real life penetrate into their cool, foggy world.

Looking at the sunset rivers where the Okkervil River also had its source, already blooming with toxic greenery, already poisoned by the living breath of an old woman, Simeonov listened to the arguing voices of two struggling demons: one demanded he throw the old woman out of his head, lock the door – opening it occasionally for Tamara – and go on as before, loving moderately, longing moderately, in moments of solitude listening to the pure sound of the silver horn singing over the unknown foggy river; the other demon, a wild youth with a mind dimmed by translating bad books, demanded that he walk, *run*, to find Vera Vasilevna, a half-blind, impoverished, emaciated, hoarse, stick-legged old woman; find her, bend over her almost deaf ear and shout through the years and misfortunes that she is the one and only, that he had passionately loved her always, that love still lives in his ailing heart, that she, the divine Peri, her voice rising from underwater depths, filling sails, speeding along the flaming waters of the night, surging upward, eclipsing half the sky, had destroyed and uplifted him – Simeonov, her faithful knight – and crushed by her silvery voice, the trolleys, books, processed cheeses, wet sidewalks, bird calls, Tamaras, cups, nameless women, passing years, and the weight of the world all rolled off like tiny pieces of gravel. And the old woman, stunned, would look at him with tear-filled eyes: What? You know me? It can't be! My God! does anyone still care? I never thought – and bewildered, she wouldn't know where to seat Simeonov, while tenderly holding her elbow and kissing her no longer white hand, covered with age spots, he would lead her to an armchair, peering into her faded face of old-fashioned bone structure. And looking at the part in her thin white hair with tenderness and pity, he would think: Oh, how we missed each other in this world. What madness that time separated us. ("Ugh, *don't*," grimaced his inner demon, but Simeonov wanted to do what was right.)

He obtained Vera Vasilevna's address in the most mundane

and insulting way – for five kopeks at a sidewalk directory kiosk. His heart thumped: would it be Okkervil? of course not. And not the embankment either. He bought chrysanthemums at the market – tiny yellow ones wrapped in cellophane. Long faded. And he picked up a cake at the bakery. The saleswoman took off the cardboard cover and showed him his selection on her outstretched hand: will it do? – but Simeonov did not notice what he was buying and recoiled, because Tamara was outside the bakery window – or was it his imagination? – going to get him, nice and warm, in his apartment. Only in the trolley did he untie his purchase and look inside. Not bad. Fruit. Decent looking. Lone fruits slept in the corners under a glassy gel: a slice of apple here; in a more expensive corner a chunk of peach; here half a plum frozen in eternal cold; here a mischievous, ladylike corner with three cherries. The sides were dusted with confectionary dandruff. The trolley jolted, the cake slipped, and Simeonov saw a clear thumbprint on the smooth jellied surface – either the careless baker's or the clumsy saleswoman's. No problem, the old woman doesn't see well. I'll cut it up right away. ("Go back" – his guardian demon sadly shook his head – "run for your life.") Simeonov retied the box as best he could and began looking at the sunset. The Okkervil rushed noisily in a narrow stream, slapping the granite shores, and the shores crumbled like sand and crept into the water. He stood before Vera Vasilevna's house, shifting the presents from hand to hand. The gates he had to pass were ornamented with a fish-scale motif. Beyond: a horrible courtyard. A cat scurried by. Just as I thought. A great forgotten artist has to live off a courtyard like this. The back entrance, garbage cans, narrow iron banisters, dirt. His heart was pounding. Long faded. *In my ailing heart.*

He rang. (*"Fool,"* said his inner demon, spat, and left Simeonov.) The door was flung open by the onslaught of noise, singing, and laughter pouring out of the apartment, and Vera Vasilevna appeared, white and huge, rouged, with thick black brows; appeared at the set table in the illuminated segment above a mound of sharply spiced hors d'oeuvres he could smell even from the doorway, above an enormous chocolate cake crowned with a chocolate bunny, laughing loudly, raucously; appeared and was selected by fate forever. He should have turned and left. Fifteen people at the table laughed, watching her: it was Vera Vasilevna's birthday, and Vera Vasilevna, gasping with laughter, was telling a joke. She had begun telling it while Simeonov was going up the stairs, she was already cheating on him with those fifteen people while he fumbled and worried at the gate, shifting the defective cake from hand to hand, while he was still in the trolley, while he was locking himself in his apartment and clearing space on his dirty table for her silvery voice, while he was taking the heavy black disc with its moonlight radiance from the yellow jacket the very first time; even before he was born, when there was only wind rustling grass and silence reigned in the world. She was not waiting for him, thin, at the lancet window, peering into the distance into the glassy streams of the Okkervil River; she was laughing in a low voice over a table crowded with dishes, over salads, cucumbers, fish, and bottles, and she drank dashingly, the enchantress, and she turned her heavy body dashingly, too. She had betrayed him. Or had he betrayed Vera Vasilevna? It was too late to figure out now.

"Another one!" someone shouted laughingly, a man, he learned immediately, with the surname Kissov. "You have to pay a fine." They took the fingerprinted cake and the flowers from Simeonov and squeezed him in at the table, making him drink to the health of Vera Vasilevna, health, as he was convinced, being the last thing she needed. Simeonov sat, smiling automatically, nodding, stabbing a pickled tomato with his fork, watching Vera Vasilevna like everyone else, listening to her loud jokes—his life was crushed, run over into two; it was his own fault, it was too late now; the magical diva had been abducted, she had allowed herself to be abducted, she hadn't given a damn about the handsome sad balding prince promised her by fate, she didn't wish to listen for his steps in the noise of the rain and the howling wind outside the autumn windowpanes, didn't wish to sleep enchanted for a hundred years after pricking her finger, she had surrounded herself with mortal, edible people, had made a friend of that horrible Kissov – made even closer, horribly, intimately, by the sound of his name – and Simeonov trampled the tall gray houses by Okkervil River, crushed the bridges with their towers and tossed away the chains, poured garbage into the clear gray water; but the river found itself a new course, and the houses stubbornly rose from the ruins, and carriages pulled by a pair of bays traveled over the bridges.

"Have a smoke?" Kissov asked. "I quit, so I don't carry any." He relieved Simeonov of half a pack. "Who are you? An adoring fan? That's good. Have your own place? With your own bath? *Gut*. She has to share one here. You'll bring her to your place to bathe. She likes to take baths. We gather on the first of the month and listen to recordings. What do you have? Have you got 'Dark Green Emerald'? Too bad. We've been looking for it for years. It's awful – nowhere to be had. The ones you have were hits, lots of them around, that's not interesting. Look for 'Emerald.' Have you any connections for getting smoked sausage? No, it's bad for her, it's for . . . me. You couldn't find any punier flowers? I brought roses, they were the size of my fist." Kissov brought his hairy fist close. "You're not a journalist, are you? It would be great to have a radio show on her, our little Vera keeps hoping for that. What a face. But her voice is still as strong as a deacon's. Let me write down your address."

He squashed Simeonov into the chair with his big hand, "Don't get up, I'll see myself out," Kissov got up from the table and left, taking Simeonov's cake with the dactyloscopic memento.

Strangers instantly inhabited the foggy banks of the Okkervil, hauling their cheap-smelling belongings – pots and mattresses, buckets and marmalade cats; there was no space on the granite embankment, they were singing their own songs, sweeping garbage onto the paving stones laid by Simeonov, giving birth, multiplying, visiting one another; the fat black-browed old woman knocked down the pale shadow with its sloping shoulders, crushed the veiled hat under her foot, and the old-fashioned round heels fell in different directions, and Vera Vasilevna shouted across the table, "Pass the mushrooms!" and Simeonov passed them and she ate some.

He watched her big nose move, and the mustache under it, watched her large black eyes veiled with a film of age travel from face to face when someone turned on a tape recorder and her silvery voice floated out, gathering strength – it's all right, thought Simeonov. I'll get home soon, it's all right. Vera Vasilevna died, she died long, long ago, killed, dismembered and eaten by this old woman, the bones were sucked clean, I could enjoy the wake but Kissov took away my cake; but it's all right, here are chrysanthemums for the grave, dry sick dead flowers, very appropriate, I've commemorated the dead, now I can get up and leave.

Tamara – the darling! – was hanging around by Simeonov's door. She picked him up, carried him in, washed him, undressed him, and fed him a hot meal. He promised Tamara he would marry her but toward morning, in his sleep, Vera Vasilevna came, spat in his face, called him names, and went down the damp embankment into the night, swaying on the black heels he had invented. In the morning Kissov knocked and rang at the door, come to examine the bathroom, to prepare it for the evening. And in the evening he brought Vera Vasilevna to bathe at Simeonov's, smoked Simeonov's cigarettes, devoured sandwiches, and said, "Ye-e-es...our little Vera is a force! Think how many men she devoured in her time – my God!" And against his will Simeonov listened to the creaks and splashes of Vera Vasilevna's heavy body in the cramped tub, how her soft, heavy, full hip pulled away from the side of the damp tub with a *slurp*, how the water drained with a sucking gurgle, how her bare feet padded on the floor and at last, throwing back the hook, out came a red parboiled Vera Vasilevna in a robe, "*Oof*. That was good." Kissov hurried with the tea, and Simeonov, enchanted, smiling, went to rinse off after Vera Vasilevna, to use the flexible shower hose to wash the gray pellets of skin from the tub's drying walls, to scoop the white hairs from the drain. Kissov wound up the gramophone, and the divine stormy voice, gaining strength, rose in a crescendo from the depths, spread its wings, soared above the world, above the steamy body of little Vera drinking tea from the saucer, above Simeonov bent in his lifelong obedience, above warm, domestic Tamara, above everyone beyond help, above the approaching sunset, the gathering rain, the wind, the nameless rivers flowing backwards, overflowing their banks, raging and flooding the city as only rivers can.

Translated by ANTONINA W. BOUIS

VII

J O R G E   L U I S   B O R G E S

The Immortals

❊   ❊   ❊   ❊   ❊

Jorge Luis Borges, the highly regarded Argentinian
writer, was born in Buenos Aires in 1899. He was
one of the main innovators of Latin American fiction, as well as a brilliant essayist and fine poet.
His works are widely available in the United States.

And see, no longer blinded by our eyes.
R U P E R T   B R O O K E

*W*HOEVER COULD HAVE FORESEEN, way back in that innocent summer of 1923, that the novelette *The Chosen One* by
Camilo N. Huergo, presented to me by the author with his personal inscription on the flyleaf (which I had the decorum to tear
out before offering the volume for sale to successive men of the
book trade), hid under the thin varnish of fiction a prophetic
truth. Huergo's photograph, in an oval frame, adorns the cover.
Each time I look at it, I have the impression that the snapshot is
about to cough, a victim of that lung disease which nipped in the
bud a promising career. Tuberculosis, in short, denied him the
happiness of acknowledging the letter I wrote him in one of my
characteristic outbursts of generosity.

The epigraph prefixed to this thoughtful essay has been taken
from the aforementioned novelette; I required Dr. Montenegro,
of the Academy, to render it into Spanish, but the results were

negative. To give the unprepared reader the gist of the matter, I shall now sketch, in condensed form, an outline of Huergo's narrative, as follows:

The storyteller pays a visit, far to the south in Chubut, to the English rancher don Guillermo Blake, who devotes his energies not only to the breeding of sheep but also to the ramblings of the world-famous Plato and to the latest and more freakish experiments in the field of surgical medicine. On the basis of his reading, don Guillermo concludes that the five senses obstruct or deform the apprehension of reality and that, could we free ourselves of them, we would see the world as it is – endless and timeless. He comes to think that the eternal models of things lie in the depths of the soul and that the organs of perception with which the Creator has endowed us are, *grosso modo*, hindrances. They are no better than dark spectacles that blind us to what exists outside, diverting our attention at the same time from the splendor we carry within us.

Blake begets a son by one of the farm girls so that the boy may one day become acquainted with reality. To anesthetize him for life, to make him blind and deaf and dumb, to emancipate him from the senses of smell and taste, were the father's first concerns. He took, in the same way, all possible measures to make the chosen one unaware of his own body. As to the rest, this was arranged with contrivances designed to take over respiration, circulation, nourishment, digestion, and elimination. It was a pity that the boy, fully liberated, was cut off from all human contact.

Owing to the press of practical matters, the narrator goes away. After ten years, he returns. Don Guillermo has died; his son goes on living after his fashion, with natural breathing, heart regular, in a dusty shack cluttered with mechanical devices. The narrator, about to leave for good, drops a cigarette butt that sets fire to the shack and he never quite knows whether this act was done on purpose or by pure chance. So ends Huergo's story,

strange enough for its time but now, of course, more than out-
stripped by the rockets and astronauts of our men of science.

Having dashed off this disinterested compendium of the tale
of a now dead and forgotten author – from whom I have nothing
to gain – I steer back to the heart of the matter. Memory restores
to me a Saturday morning in 1964 when I had an appointment
with the eminent gerontologist Dr. Raúl Narbondo. The sad
truth is that we young bloods of yesteryear are getting on; the
thick mop begins to thin, one or another ear stops up, the wrinkles collect grime, molars grow hollow, a cough takes root, the
backbone hunches up, the foot trips on a pebble, and to put it
plainly, the paterfamilias falters and withers. There was no
doubt about it, the moment had come to see Dr. Narbondo for a
general checkup, particularly considering the fact that he spe-
cialized in the replacement of malfunctioning organs.

Sick at heart because that afternoon the Palermo Juniors and
the Spanish Sports were playing a return match and maybe I
could not occupy my place in the front row to bolster my team, I
betook myself to the clinic on Corrientes Avenue near Pasteur.
The clinic, as its fame betrays, occupies the fifteenth floor of the
Adamant Building. I went up by elevator (manufactured by the
Electra Company). Eye to eye with Narbondo's brass shingle, I
pressed the bell, and at long last, taking my courage in both
hands, I slipped through the partly open door and entered into
the waiting room proper. There, alone with the latest issues of
the *Ladies' Companion* and *Jumbo*, I whiled away the passing
hours until a cuckoo clock struck twelve and sent me leaping
from my armchair. At once, I asked myself, What happened?
Planning my every move now like a sleuth, I took a step or two
toward the next room, peeped in, ready, admittedly, to fly the
coop at the slightest sound. From the streets far below came the
noise of horns and traffic, the cry of a newspaper hawker, the
squeal of brakes sparing some pedestrian, but, all around me, a
reign of silence. I crossed a kind of laboratory, or pharmaceutical

back room, furnished with instruments and flasks of all sorts. Stimulated by the aim of reaching the men's room, I pushed open a door at the far end of the lab.

Inside, I saw something that my eyes did not understand. The small enclosure was circular, painted white, with a low ceiling and neon lighting, and without a single window to relieve the sense of claustrophobia. The room was inhabited by four personages, or pieces of furniture. Their color was the same as the walls, their material wood, their form cubic. On each cube was another small cube with a latticed opening and below it a slot as in a mailbox. Carefully scrutinizing the grilled opening, you noted with alarm that from the interior you were being watched by something like eyes. The slots emitted, from time to time, a chorus of sighs or whisperings that the good Lord himself could not have made head or tail of. The placement of these cubes was such that they faced each other in the form of a square, composing a kind of conclave. I don't know how many minutes lapsed. At this point, the doctor came in and said to me, "My pardon, Bustos, for having kept you waiting. I was just out getting myself an advance ticket for today's match between the Palermo Juniors and the Spanish Sports." He went on, indicating the cubes, "Let me introduce you to Santiago Silberman, to retired clerk-of-court Ludueña, to Aquiles Molinari, and to Miss Bugard."

Out of the furniture came faint rumbling sounds. I quickly reached out a hand and, without the pleasure of shaking theirs, withdrew in good order, a frozen smile on my lips. Reaching the vestibule as best I could, I managed to stammer, "A drink. A stiff drink."

Narbondo came out of the lab with a graduated beaker filled with water and dissolved some effervescent drops into it. Blessed concoction – the wretched taste brought me to my senses. Then, the door to the small room closed and locked tight, came the explanation:

"I'm glad to see, my dear Bustos, that my immortals have

made quite an impact on you. Whoever would have thought that *Homo sapiens*, Darwin's barely human ape, could achieve such perfection? This, my house, I assure you, is the only one in all Indo-America where Dr. Eric Stapledon's methodology has been fully applied. You recall, no doubt, the consternation that the death of the late lamented doctor, which took place in New Zealand, occasioned in scientific circles. I flatter myself, furthermore, for having implemented his precursory labors with a few Argentinean touches. In itself, the thesis – Newton's apple all over again – is fairly simple. The death of the body is a result, always, of the failure of some organ or other, call it the kidney, lungs, heart, or what you like. With the replacement of the organism's various components, in themselves perishable, with other corresponding stainless or polyethylene parts, there is no earthly reason whatever why the soul, why you yourself – Bustos Domecq – should not be immortal. None of your philosophical niceties here; the body can be vulcanized and from time to time recaulked, and so the mind keeps going. Surgery brings immortality to mankind. Life's essential aim has been attained – the mind lives on without fear of cessation. Each of our immortals is comforted by the certainty, backed by our firm's guarantee, of being a witness *in aeternum*. The brain, refreshed night and day by a system of electrical charges, is the last organic bulwark in which ball bearings and cells collaborate. The rest is Formica, steel, plastics. Respiration, alimentation, generation, mobility – elimination itself! – belong to the past. Our immortal is real estate. One or two minor touches are still missing, it's true. Oral articulation, dialogue, may still be improved. As for the costs, you need not worry yourself. By means of a procedure that circumvents legal red tape, the candidate transfers his property to us, and the Narbondo Company, Inc. – I, my son, his descendants – guarantees your upkeep, *in statu quo*, to the end of time. And, I might add, a moneyback guarantee."

It was then that he laid a friendly hand on my shoulder. I felt his will taking power over me. "Ha-ha! I see I've whetted your appetite, I've tempted you, dear Bustos. You'll need a couple of months or so to get your affairs in order and to have your stock portfolio signed over to us. As far as the operation goes, naturally, as a friend, I want to save you a little something. Instead of our usual fee of ten thousand dollars, for you, ninety-five hundred – in cash, of course. The rest is yours. It goes to pay your lodging, care, and service. The medical procedure in itself is painless. No more than a question of amputation and replacement. Nothing to worry about. On the eve, just keep yourself calm, untroubled. Avoid heavy meals, tobacco, and alcohol, apart from your accustomed and imported, I hope, Scotch or two. Above all, refrain from impatience."

"Why two months?" I asked him. "One's enough, and then some. I come out of the anesthesia and I'm one more of your cubes. You have my address and phone number. We'll keep in touch. I'll be back next Friday at the latest."

At the escape hatch he handed me the card of Nemirovski, Nemirovski, & Nemirovski, Counsellors at Law, who would put themselves at my disposal for all the details of drawing up the will. With perfect composure I walked to the subway entrance, then took the stairs at a run. I lost no time. That same night, without leaving the slightest trace behind, I moved to the New Impartial, in whose register I figure under the assumed name of Aquiles Silberman. Here, in my bedroom at the far rear of this modest hotel, wearing a false beard and dark spectacles, I am setting down this account of the facts.

Translated by NORMAN THOMAS DI GIOVANNI
With ADOLFO BIOY-CASARES

J A M A I C A   K I N C A I D

My Mother

✳   ✳   ✳   ✳   ✳

Jamaica Kincaid's most recent book is *Lucy*. She is also the author of *At the Bottom of the River* and *Annie John*. She was born in St. John's, Antigua and now lives in Bennington, VT.

*I*MMEDIATELY on wishing my mother dead and seeing the pain it caused her, I was sorry and cried so many tears that all the earth around me was drenched. Standing before my mother, I begged her forgiveness, and I begged so earnestly that she took pity on me, kissing my face and placing my head on her bosom to rest. Placing her arms around me, she drew my head closer and closer to her bosom, until finally I suffocated. I lay on her bosom, breathless, for a time uncountable, until one day, for a reason she has kept to herself, she shook me out and stood me under a tree and I started to breathe again. I cast a sharp glance at her and said to myself, "So." Instantly I grew my own bosoms, small mounds at first, leaving a small, soft place between them, where, if ever necessary, I could rest my own head. Between my mother and me now were the tears I had cried, and I gathered up some stones and banked them in so that they formed a small pond. The water in the pond was thick and black and poisonous, so that only unnamable invertebrates could live in it. My mother and I now watched each other carefully, always making sure to shower the other with words and deeds of love and affection.

I WAS SITTING on my mother's bed trying to get a good look at myself. It was a large bed and it stood in the middle of a large, completely dark room. The room was completely dark because all the windows had been boarded up and all the crevices stuffed with black cloth. My mother lit some candles and the room burst into a pinklike, yellowlike glow. Looming over us, much larger than ourselves, were our shadows. We sat mesmerized because our shadows had made a place between themselves, as if they were making room for someone else. Nothing filled up the space between them, and the shadow of my mother sighed. The shadow of my mother danced around the room to a tune that my own shadow sang, and then they stopped. All along, our shadows had grown thick and thin, long and short, had fallen at every angle, as if they were controlled by the light of day. Suddenly my mother got up and blew out the candles and our shadows vanished. I continued to sit on the bed, trying to get a good look at myself.

MY MOTHER removed her clothes and covered thoroughly her skin with a thick gold-colored oil, which had recently been rendered in a hot pan from the livers of reptiles with pouched throats. She grew plates of metal-colored scales on her back, and light, when it collided with this surface, would shatter and collapse into tiny points. Her teeth now arranged themselves into rows that reached all the way back to her long white throat. She uncoiled her hair from her head and then removed her hair altogether. Taking her head into her large palms, she flattened it so that her eyes, which were by now ablaze, sat on top of her head and spun like two revolving balls. Then, making two lines on the soles of each foot, she divided her feet into crossroads. Silently, she had instructed me to follow her example, and now I too traveled along on my white underbelly, my tongue darting and flickering in the hot air. "Look," said my mother.

MY MOTHER and I were standing on the seabed side by side, my arms laced loosely around her waist, my head resting securely on her shoulder, as if I needed the support. To make sure she believed in my frailness, I sighed occasionally – long soft sighs, the kind of sigh she had long ago taught me could evoke sympathy. In fact, how I really felt was invincible. I was no longer a child but I was not yet a woman. My skin had just blackened and cracked and fallen away and my new impregnable carapace had taken full hold. My nose had flattened; my hair curled in and stood out straight from my head simultaneously; my many rows of teeth in their retractable trays were in place. My mother and I wordlessly made an arrangement – I sent out my beautiful sighs, she received them; I leaned ever more heavily on her for support, she offered her shoulder, which shortly grew to the size of a thick plank. A long time passed, at the end of which I had hoped to see my mother permanently cemented to the seabed. My mother reached out to pass a hand over my head, a pacifying gesture, but I laughed and, with great agility, stepped aside. I let out a horrible roar, then a self-pitying whine. I had grown big, but my mother was bigger, and that would always be so. We walked to the Garden of Fruits and there ate to our hearts' satisfaction. We departed through the southwesterly gate, leaving as always, in our trail, small colonies of worms.

WITH MY MOTHER, I crossed, unwillingly, the valley. We saw a lamb grazing and when it heard our footsteps it paused and looked up at us. The lamb looked cross and miserable. I said to my mother, "The lamb is cross and miserable. So would I be, too, if I had to live in a climate not suited to my nature." My mother and I now entered the cave. It was the dark and cold cave. I felt something growing under my feet and I bent down to eat it. I stayed that way for years, bent over eating whatever I found growing under my feet. Eventually, I grew a special lens that would allow me to see in the darkest of darkness; eventually, I grew a special coat that kept me warm in the coldest of coldness. One day I saw my mother sitting on a rock. She said, "What a strange expression you have on your face. So cross, so miserable, as if you were living in a climate not suited to your nature." Laughing, she vanished. I dug a deep, deep hole. I built a beautiful house, a floorless house, over the deep, deep hole. I put in lattice windows, most favored of windows by my mother, so perfect for looking out at people passing by without her being observed. I painted the house itself yellow, the windows green, colors I knew would please her. Standing just outside the door, I asked her to inspect the house. I said, "Take a look. Tell me if it's to your satisfaction." Laughing out of the corner of a mouth I could not see, she stepped inside. I stood just outside the door, listening carefully, hoping to hear her land with a thud at the bottom of the deep, deep hole. Instead, she walked up and down in every direction, even pounding her heel on the air. Coming outside to greet me, she said, "It is an excellent house. I would be honored to live in it," and then vanished. I filled up the hole and burnt the house to the ground.

MY MOTHER has grown to an enormous height. I have grown to an enormous height also, but my mother's height is three times mine. Sometimes I cannot see from her breasts on up, so lost is she in the atmosphere. One day, seeing her sitting on the seashore, her hand reaching out in the deep to caress the belly of a striped fish as he swam through a place where two seas met, I glowed red with anger. For a while then I lived alone on the island where there were eight full moons and I adorned the face of each moon with expressions I had seen on my mother's face. All the expressions favored me. I soon grew tired of living in this way and returned to my mother's side. I remained, though glowing red with anger, and my mother and I built houses on opposite banks of the dead pond. The dead pond lay between us; in it, only small invertebrates with poisonous lances lived. My mother behaved toward them as if she had suddenly found herself in the same room with relatives we had long since risen above. I cherished their presence and gave them names. Still I missed my mother's close company and cried constantly for her, but at the end of each day when I saw her return to her house, incredible and great deeds in her wake, each of them singing loudly her praises, I glowed and glowed again, red with anger. Eventually, I wore myself out and sank into a deep, deep sleep, the only dreamless sleep I have ever had.

ONE DAY my mother packed my things in a grip and, taking me by the hand, walked me to the jetty, placed me on board a boat, in care of the captain. My mother, while caressing my chin and cheeks, said some words of comfort to me because we had never been apart before. She kissed me on the forehead and turned and walked away. I cried so much my chest heaved up and down, my whole body shook at the sight of her back turned toward me, as if I had never seen her back turned toward me before. I started to make plans to get off the boat, but when I saw that the boat was encased in a large green bottle, as if it were about to decorate a mantelpiece, I fell asleep, until I reached my destination, the new island. When the boat stopped, I got off and I saw a woman with feet exactly like mine, especially around the arch of the instep. Even though the face was completely different from what I was used to, I recognized this woman as my mother. We greeted each other at first with great caution and politeness, but as we walked along, our steps became one, and as we talked, our voices became one voice, and we were in complete union in every other way. What peace came over me then, for I could not see where she left off and I began, or where I left off and she began.

MY MOTHER and I walk through the rooms of her house. Every crack in the floor holds a significant event: here, an apparently healthy young man suddenly dropped dead; here, a young woman defied her father and, while riding her bicycle to the forbidden lovers' meeting place, fell down a precipice, remaining a cripple for the rest of a very long life. My mother and I find this a beautiful house. The rooms are large and empty, opening on to each other, waiting for people and things to fill them up. Our white muslin skirts billow up around our ankles, our hair hangs straight down our backs as our arms hang straight at our sides. I fit perfectly in the crook of my mother's arm, on the curve of her back, in the hollow of her stomach. We eat from the same bowl, drink from the same cup; when we sleep, our heads rest on the same pillow. As we walk through the rooms, we merge and separate, merge and separate; soon we shall enter the final stage of our evolution.

THE FISHERMEN are coming in from sea; their catch is bountiful, my mother has seen to that. As the waves plop, plop against each other, the fishermen are happy that the sea is calm. My mother points out the fishermen to me, their contentment is a source of my contentment. I am sitting in my mother's enormous lap. Sometimes I sit on a mat she has made for me from her hair. The lime trees are weighed down with limes – I have already perfumed myself with their blossoms. A hummingbird has nested on my stomach, a sign of my fertileness. My mother and I live in a bower made from flowers whose petals are imperishable. There is the silvery blue of the sea, crisscrossed with sharp darts of light, there is the warm rain falling on the clumps of castor bush, there is the small lamb bounding across the pasture, there is the soft ground welcoming the soles of my pink feet. It is in this way my mother and I have lived for a long time now.

The Concert

✳   ✳   ✳   ✳   ✳

Julio Ricci, one of Uruguay's most important and
prolific writers, lives in Montevideo where, until his
recent retirement, he taught linguistics. His only
publication in English is *Falling Through
the Cracks*.

I'VE JUST THOROUGHLY RINSED my mouth with a liquid
that came highly recommended to me and which really soothes
my throat. I'm sure that some of my friends are doing the same
thing at this very moment. Friends? What friends?...I hardly
even know them! They're a bunch of senior citizens even older
than I am, or a bunch of old folks even more senior than I am,
who sit next to me on those broken-down chairs that are almost
black with age, and laugh without knowing why.

Obviously, times change and technology is creating new and
previously unimagined professions. Carpentry, blacksmithing,
tailoring and so many other biblical trades will soon disappear.
In the future, readers of the Bible will have to take special
courses to understand these things.

Well, maybe what my contemporaries and I do doesn't consti-
tute a trade or a profession. It is an as-yet unnamed activity performed by people like us who can't do anything else any longer.
Or rather, by people like us who can't do anything more than de-

mand almost nothing as pay and accept the crumbs they throw us.

I must confess that there was a time when I was impressed by the phrase from a tango: "...and not think about myself any more." I was impressed because at that time, and until very recently, I'd actually stopped thinking about myself. Just like everyone else. Who stops to think about himself? What you think about are your daily problems, but not yourself. That's the luxury of philosophers.

Yesterday I laughed a lot, which is not the same as saying I had a good laugh. However, the director told us our output was poor, that we had to produce heartier laughs and louder guffaws. He informed us that he had made a computerized market survey and that the computer had indicated that the stronger the laughter, the greater the audience stimulation, the greater the comedian's success, and the greater the television channel's profits.

He didn't say a word about raising our salaries even ten cents. The minimum wage was sufficient; this seemed to be the tacit statement. What he did say was that we would do well to protect our positions. In other words, he threatened us.

It's been horribly cold since last week, and I find it hard to get up early, wash, shave, and have my coffee. Those cold blasts whipping up out of Patagonia are bad for my health. At the bus stop I have to stand there shivering and trying to breathe in the face of some really fierce winds. By the time the bus comes along I'm stiff with cold.

The six hours of work at the TV station are exhausting. Who would imagine that while so many people work with their hands or their brains, others do it—we do it—with laughter. That's right: we sell laughs. No one would imagine that laughs, yuks, are today a marketable product, that there is a laugh market and that this market even has its prices quoted on the stock exchange. A little while ago I wouldn't have thought that at this stage of my life—I've seen seventy-four Christmases come and go—I would end up in this profession. It's only the simple exercise, or the simple exploitation, of a condition natural to man. (An animal would never make a living on laughter.)

The director informed us that on May 10 the channel would present a comedian of great international renown – a Julio Iglesias or a Pelé or a Ronald Reagan of the joke and the pun – and that we had to be prepared to laugh "mightily," and, if possible, to duly prolong our peals of laughter, like the great tenors, I suppose. He told us he had even hired backup laughter personnel, and that he was going to test their abilities. He said that if they turn out to be better than we are, we'll be relieved of our duties.

Perhaps as a result of this employment, or para-employment, I often find myself thinking about myself. The truth is that the pettiness of life, the narrowness of daily routine – getting up and lying down, eating, earning a living, defecating, in other words, all those things that parade before our senses daily – distract attention from our innermost selves and inhibit us from thinking. I've always lived wrapped up in those things, perhaps like Rockefeller, like Reagan, like the Pope, always organizing "exteriorities": the world banking crisis, the struggles for democracy, social contacts, etc. And I've given very little time to thinking about my own nothingness.

The day before yesterday the elderly laugher sitting next to me was feeling ill. He had launched a volley of hoarse, peculiar peals of laughter and then suddenly passed out: he deflated, you might say, and fell to the floor. They left him there a while, stretched out on the floor. His eyes were closed. It was not possible to interrupt the comedian. The block of time, more important than the old man, had to be filled. The director had him placed on a stretcher immediately after the time was up.

"Get that old man out of here," he said.

He was taken away and immediately replaced by a substitute who was equally old, but uglier and almost a dwarf. Nothing more was ever heard of the other man. He was history and had no importance. The show – that is, the present – had to go on, period. I did notice, however, that the new old man, the dwarf, laughed with enormous stridency. You could tell he had a terrific constitution.

I think that the new practice of calibrating the decibel level of our laughter is going too far. But what can you do? Everything is technified and quantified and paid for these days.

I haven't told anyone about it, but I'm training myself, or simply training, as they say nowadays, at home. I'm trying to increase the volume of my laughter. The truth is that I've never been much of a laugher, let alone someone who would split a gut laughing. In fact, there were those who labeled me as sad. I never thought that one day I would end up, not just doing piecework laughs, but even worrying about my style of laughter, of guffaws, and studying the various types of laughter. And even less that I'd end up classifying them by their duration, their decibel level, their tone. Today I know that there are provocative laughs, laughs which are sexually arousing, ironic laughs, bestial laughs, brutal and even erotic laughs. There is a whole gamut of ways to laugh, and I'm sure that one day German scientists will write the *Treatise on Laughter* or *Grundriss des Lachens*. And the Americans will evaluate them all in their economic and monetary aspects (free floating, basic cash reserves, projected growth, etc.), and the Japanese will commercialize them in the form of calibrating mechanisms and will even manufacture laughing robots.

I'm worried about the arrival of the great comedian from Spain. I foresee that we present laughers will all have to outdo ourselves at that time. We'll have to employ all our ebbing pulmonary strength, stretch our vocal cords to the limit, and put on our most cheerful party faces to keep our jobs.

I've just noticed something that strikes me as odd. They're setting up what looks like traffic lights facing our work area. One of the many bigwigs who come and go at the television station said that these are the lights the director is going to use. Red will mean *silence*; yellow will mean *get ready*; and green will be the signal to burst out laughing. The man doesn't want to have to use his hands anymore.

Lately I've noticed that this job's routine is even changing our personalities. The other day, the director had a word with one of the laughers, old González, seventy-seven years of age. He was entirely serious, pointing out González's faults, and his habit of laughing at the wrong time. The old man, instead of paying attention to the director, agreeing and thanking him, began to laugh uproariously. It was as though his brakes had failed and he couldn't stop. I myself, whenever I go to the store or talk to anyone, can't help laughing. Not even the economic crisis or Denmark's six-to-one soccer victory (I'm a Uruguayan) stops me. I'm conscious of this, so I make a great effort to prevent it. And I turn my face to the side, take out a handkerchief, and pretend to sneeze and cough when I laugh.

I'm impressed, or maybe it would be more accurate to say I am unimpressed, by the behavior of the great comedians. People who see them flaunt themselves and show off in order to produce an atmosphere of merriment and uproar are convinced that these comics are on the ball. They think they're happy-go-lucky, friendly guys who let their hair down and get familiar with everyone and kid around with people. But they're really nothing at all like that. When they arrive, we old folks are already waiting there in our chairs, our laughter at the ready to encourage them, to cheer them on. And out of all these comics, not one ever deigned even to look at us. In fact, we're just like the furniture, the carpets, and the other inanimate objects that comprise the set. We're props or even less. When their act is over, they disconnect their jovial faces, plug in their serious faces, and leave, stone-faced, without even glancing at anyone. The comic turns into the anti-comic. Some of them have hellish tempers and will swear like troopers for the least little thing.

The truth is that because it's our job to laugh and to concentrate on our work, we no longer pay any attention to the jokes. Besides, when you become familiar with the whole repertoire of television jokes these comedians have, you realize it's something like one single mold into which some new material is poured. It's basically a sort of mechanical exercise based on puns and crude vulgarities. But people go for all that. They love hearing vulgarities over and over. My colleagues, the "laugh aids," do nothing but wait for the green light (laugh) or the red light (cease laughing) from the director. They've even stopped thinking. Sometimes, and I include myself, it's hard for us to stop laughing. After all, we produce laughter for a period of more than thirty seconds, and we fall victim to inertia. We lose control and keep right on laughing. The director becomes furious and even curses. He has a certain Toscanini-like air about him; all he lacks is talent. In other words, he possesses all the attributes of a great conductor – the balding head, the energy, the seriousness of purpose, the capacity for insult – but no orchestra. Conducting laughter is not the same as conducting the symphony orchestra of a great concert hall. Still, if he were skilled, he'd be able to lend a certain choirlike flavor to the group. But it's obvious that he's not. All he thinks about are the lights, about mechanical things, just as we do.

Yesterday he called me and another laugher over, and told us our laughter had a very low level of resonance. It didn't reach the established decibel level. He threatened to fire us and to take on any one of the ninety candidates (retirees) who are waiting for their turn, i.e., are waiting for one of us to die. He lost his temper, shouted and even became disheveled as he waved his arms about like a symphony orchestra conductor, but minus the orchestra.

The fact is that we're all old, or rather a bunch of old folks, which is not the same thing. I don't know why they don't hire young people. The youngest old person is a seventy-two-year-old wraith who weighs no more than 120 pounds. A certain Pérez Galindo or Galindo Pérez. The oldest oldster is an old lady of eighty-two years of age, Doña Juanita.

While we were waiting for the bus, Pérez told me that there are times when he doesn't feel well, that he suffers from heart problems, but that at this stage of the game he can't afford to give up his job because he couldn't live on his retirement income. I don't know how long I can keep it up. Where there's life there's hope. It's all going to depend on my gargling, my training program and, absolutely, on the decibel level of my laughter.

I practice a lot at night. I'm trying to raise the volume of my laughter. I do this in front of the bathroom mirror. I look at myself just as I am when I laugh. It's not like Borges' mirrors, filled with the mysteries of the Kabbala, with gardens of forking paths and with metaphysics. It's a mirror of primary and superficial properties. A mirror that shows how my veins swell, shows a mouth with unsteady false teeth (I can't afford new dentures). It shows the saliva that at times sprays the glass surface. What I really would like would be a mirror that would show the way I looked as a young man. But it hasn't been invented yet. Maybe sometime in the future they'll invent a retrospective, or rather, rejuvenating mirror.

I never imagined the world would come to this degree of competition. At my age I'm like young men competing for careers, building their muscles, etc. I'm sure that in spite of everything I'll improve. I'll turn out bigger and better laughs.

I haven't done badly with this job. I've made new friends and I've broken away from the confines of my little room's four walls. I've launched an incredible social life. Little old Juanita invited me to her room for tea and to witness her different styles of laughter. Well, what else could she invite me to? She gave me a demonstration of laughs in several tones and told me all about the ups and downs of her extensive love life while we had a few cups of tea. She's in pretty good condition despite her age.

Juanita has arrived at this stage of her life with not much to show for it. Well, at a certain point in life, human beings gradually get rid of almost everything. Material goods lose their meaning. The poor woman makes do with very little, as elderly folks do. She has a miniscule bed, a little table with a kerosene stove, a kettle, and one chair. The walls are virgin; there's nothing hanging on them. If she were a man, she'd at least have a photo of the Peñarol Soccer Team, or their rival, the Nacional Team, maybe from the thirties, or a photo of Carlos Gardel, the great tango singer of years gone by. But there's nothing there. On a small shelf or bracket—and this is all there is—there are some faded photographs. A man and a woman. And also some prints of the Virgin Mary and of Jesus on the cross. All these things, memories, help her go on with her long life. It was very cold, and Juanita was wrapped in a coat of mangy fur that made me think of the ermine stole in the tango of the same name.

"This profession, if that's the right term, will never become unionized," she commented. "It's a step lower than that of prostitutes, who are already unionized in some countries. Our struggle will always have to be individual. To the death."

"You're right," I agreed.

Don Juan I, there are two other Juans (luckily my name is José) asked me to visit him, too. He wanted to speak to me about the great comedian who'd be coming soon, the Pelé or Julio Iglesias or Sinatra of jokes. The "Messiah of Jokedom," as he called him. He told me how he imagined him to be. He would be a real gentleman, very Spanish, very continental, very kind. He would shake hands with each and every one of us and would lavish on us his great affection and warmth, the affection and warmth of a great maestro. He wouldn't be like our local comics.

Don Juan I began to speak in great circumlocutions, periphrastically beating around the bush in ever-widening circles until I couldn't tell where he was coming from or where he was heading. Finally, when it was time to leave and I stood up, he

ended his conceptual bush-beating and his deviosities and managed to say something less muddled. He told me he had a great
surprise in store for the comedian.

Once more I looked around at Juan I's miserable little room.
Juan I, my contemporary, skinny, ugly, poor, and generally
beat-up. His entire world was composed of two chairs that were
falling apart, a bed that was actually a cot, a Bulgarian kerosene
stove, a three-legged table that was short and squat, plus a pot, a
kettle, and the utensils used for brewing and drinking the indis-
pensable *maté*. There wasn't even a guitar anywhere or even
cookies on the table, but I did see little bottles of medication and
some used corn plasters.

"Yes, I have a great surprise for him," he said, and then burst
out with two peals of laughter for practice.

I went downstairs in the dark of the night, almost having to
grope my way along, and came to Baldomero Fernández Ro-
mero, the street named for the poet, and the corner of either Laguna or Pergamino – I'm not sure which – to take the bus.

The great day arrived. The comic's name was Radamés
Dilurio or Delugeo or Diluvian. Just like all his fellow comedians, he didn't even glance at us. We were nothing more than
some five hundred or six hundred combined years of veteran or
veterinary or vegetable entities installed in rows of chairs. We
were preparing our throats and making muffled, indefinable
noises. We were tuning up our instruments as musicians do in
concert halls. The hum of our vocal cords could be heard in their
pre-warm-up state.

Supercomic Dilurio strode forward, Mussolini-like, and
plugged in his beaming face, activacting the facial muscles that
produce the conventional smile mechanisms. He selected one of
the faces on his program: that of a pampered idiot. It was obvious he was master of an entire repertoire of facial expressions: we
could see this immediately. It ranged from the nuance of a lively
fool to that of a hopeless idiot. In other words, he had at his com-

mand the entire infinite range of tele-hilarious and tele-sensitive touches. He was a blend of Charlie Chaplin, Sid Caesar, Buster Keaton, Bob Hope, Milton Burlesque, Rodney Dangerfield, and Eddie Murphy. He went from an expression of boredom to one of fatigue, of rage, of joy, or enchantment, of eroticism *con fuoco* à la Red Foxx, and of chaste bashfulness. He went through the entire range with which thirty centuries of theatrical necessity have endowed humanity.

He started his collection of jokes. The whole program was based on famous telegrams. The audience began to laugh, and we started our accompaniment. I had never seen my colleagues so excited. It was like a key soccer match, like a world final or one with a high score between, let's say, Denmark and Uruguay. The ball was passed back and forth, and the people roared with excitement. It was wonderful.

The second batch of jokes started with the kind that could be called pornographic. Jokes, that is, in tune with the times. But it was cybernetic pornography. How would the machines of the future make love? What was the lovemaking style of Japanese robots? How would computers reproduce?

There was a moment in which Dilurio the Great had all his transistors in operation, his face contorted with eroticism, and everyone's spirits soaring. At this moment Don Juan I stood up, emerged from the obscurity of the laugh team, positioned himself center stage, and began to laugh. The lighting crew, not knowing what was happening, illuminated his face and body in lights of every color. They practically bathed him in color.

Suddenly there was soft music. Don Juan I began to emit peals of laughter. He passed from one type of laughter to another, from a *do*, to a *re*, to a *mi*, and so on. He utilized every nuance imaginable: laughter that was violent, soft, savage, grotesque, intelligent, miniscule, gigantic. He was a complete concert of unimaginable laughter and was such a spectacle that the comedian, the telegrams, the eroticism, had all passed into the past. Into the most remote past. Don Juan I was growing larger than life. It was an ineffable music of laughter in G-flat, which at times recalled the melodies of Beethoven, of Bach, of Borodin. The laugh concert drew the chorus of oldsters into it, and they too started to laugh uproariously.

Finally, Don Juan I, who was no longer Don Juan I, but the King of Belly Laughs and Guffaws, found the lost chord. At that moment he fell as though struck by lightning. The asinine world-class comedian didn't know what to do. The director had disappeared, and the audience was one rollicking mass of laughter. The light continued to bathe the supine body for several seconds and then switched off. Don Juan I was dying happily and with laughter on his lips. He had outshined Dilurio the Great.

Translated by CLARK M. ZLOTCHEW

ACKNOWLEDGMENTS

HENNIE AUCAMP. "Soup for the Sick" is from *Home Visits*, edited and translated by Ian Ferguson. Copyright © 1983 by Tafelberg Publishers Ltd. Reprinted by permission of Tafelberg Publishers Ltd. (Cape Town, RSA).

JORGE LUIS BORGES. "The Immortals" is from *The Aleph and Other Stories* by Jorge Luis Borges. English translation copyright © 1970 by Jorge Luis Borges, Adolfo Bioy-Casares, and Norman Thomas di Giovanni. Reprinted by permission of the publisher, Dutton, an imprint of New American Library, a division of Penguin Books USA Inc.

MARGARETA EKSTRÖM. "Lilies of the Valley" is from *The Day I Began My Studies in Philosophy*, edited by Eva Claeson, is translated by Eva Claeson. Original stories and translation are copyright © 1989 by the author and translator, respectively. Reprinted by permission of White Pine Press (Fredonia, NY).

MAVIS GALLANT. "His Mother" is from *From the Fifteenth District*. Copyright © 1973, 1974, 1975, 1976, 1977, 1978, 1979 by Mavis Gallant. Reprinted by permission of Georges Borchardt, Inc. for the author.

MAURICE GEE. "A Glorious Morning, Comrade" is from *Collected Stories* (Penguin). Copyright © 1975, 1986 by Maurice Gee. Reprinted by permission of Richards Literary Agency, Auckland.

RUTH PRAWER JHABVALA. "The Man with the Dog" is from *Out of India: Selected Stories*. Copyright © 1986 by R.P. Jhabvala. Reprinted by permission of William Morrow & Co., Inc.

ELIZABETH JOLLEY. "The Pear Tree Dance" is from *Woman in a Lampshade*. Copyright © 1972, 1976, 1978, 1979, 1981, 1982 by Elizabeth Jolley. Reprinted by permission of Penguin Books Australia, Ltd.

JONATHAN KARIARA. "Her Warrior" is from *Modern African Prose* (Heinemann Educational Books, Ltd., 1967), edited by Richard Rive. Copyright © 1966 by Richard Rive. Reprinted by permission of Leonard du Plooy and the Estate of Richard Rive.

YASUNARI KAWABATA. "The Neighbors" is excerpted from *Palm-of-the-Hand Stories* by Yasunari Kawabata, English translation copyright © 1988 by Lane Dunlop and J. Martin Holman. Published by North Point Press and reprinted by permission.

MOHAMMED KHUDAYYIR. "Clocks Like Horses" is from *Arabic Short Stories*, translated by Denys Johnson-Davies, and published by Quartet Books (U.K.). Copyright © 1983 by Denys Johnson-Davies. Reprinted by permission.

JAMAICA KINCAID. "My Mother" is from *At the Bottom of the River* by Jamaica Kincaid. Copyright © 1978, 1979, 1981, 1982, 1983 by Jamaica Kincaid. Reprinted by permission of Farrar, Straus and Giroux, Inc.

TOSHIO MORI. "The Man with Bulging Pockets" is from *The Chauvinist and Other Stories* by Toshio Mori. Copyright © 1979 by the University of California, Los Angeles. Reprinted by permission of the author's estate and the Asian American Studies Center, UCLA.

This book was designed by Tree Swenson.

The Imprint type was set by Typeworks.

This book was manufactured by Edwards Brothers

on acid-free paper.

OTHER BOOKS IN
THE GRAYWOLF SHORT FICTION SERIES

Paulette Bates Alden / *Feeding the Eagles*

Paulé Bartón / *The Woe Shirt*

H.E. Bates / *My Uncle Silas*

Geri Chavis, ed. / *Family: Stories from the Interior*

Sharon Doubiago / *The Book of Seeing with One's Own Eyes*

Miriam Dow & Jennifer Regan, eds. /
The Invisible Enemy: Alcoholism & the Modern Short Story

Abby Frucht / *Fruit of the Month*

Joseph Geha / *Through and Through: Toledo Stories*

Mavis Gallant / *The Pegnitz Junction*

Patricia Henley / *Friday Night at Silver Star*

Jim Heynen / *The Man Who Kept Cigars in His Cap*

Kathrine Jason, ed. & trans. /*Name & Tears & Other Stories:*
Forty Years of Italian Fiction

Laura Kalpakian / *Fair Augusto & Other Stories*

Weldon Kees / *The Ceremony & Other Stories*

William Kittredge / *We Are Not in This Together*

Ella Leffland / *Last Courtesies & Other Stories*

David Quammen / *Blood Line: Stories of Fathers and Sons*

Mercè Rodoreda / *My Christina & Other Stories*

Dorothy Sennett, ed. /
Full Measure: Modern Short Stories on Aging

Kathleen Spivack / *The Honeymoon*

Scott Walker, ed. / *The Graywolf Annual: Short Stories*

Scott Walker, ed. / *The Graywolf Annual 2: Short Stories by Women*

Scott Walker, ed. / *The Graywolf Annual 4: Short Stories by Men*

Scott Walker, ed. / *The Graywolf Annual 6:*
Stories from the Rest of the World

Scott Walker, ed. / *The Graywolf Annual 7:*
Stories from the American Mosaic

Will Weaver / *A Gravestone Made of Wheat*